SpringerBriefs in Accounting

Series editors

More information about this series at http://www.springer.com/series/11900

Carmen Olsen

A Study of Professional Skepticism

Springer

Carmen Olsen
Department of Accounting,
Auditing and Law
Norwegian School of Economics
Bergen
Norway

ISSN 2196-7873 ISSN 2196-7881 (electronic)
SpringerBriefs in Accounting
ISBN 978-3-319-49895-9 ISBN 978-3-319-49896-6 (eBook)
DOI 10.1007/978-3-319-49896-6

Library of Congress Control Number: 2016963289

Printed on acid-free paper

This Springer imprint is published by Springer Nature
The registered company is Springer International Publishing AG
The registered company address is: Gewerbestrasse 11, 6330 Cham, Switzerland

Preface

I was first fascinated by skepticism (one way to define it is being alert) for a long time ago when I was figuring out my way into life and standing alone in a world full of opportunities and threats. I discovered that skepticism is a professional attitude when I studied to be an accountant. While working shortly as an accountant, I understood that being continuously alert is difficult, still it was important and required in accounting.

In 2010, I wrote a Ph.D. proposal on auditors' professional skepticism and was accepted in the Ph.D. program at the Norwegian School of Economics. *A Study of Professional Skepticism* is based on my Ph.D. thesis accomplished in June 2015.

Bergen, Norway Carmen Olsen

Contents

1 Auditors' Professional Skepticism 1
- 1.1 About the Book 1
- 1.2 Professional Skepticism 3
- 1.3 Institutional Settings in Norway 4
- 1.4 Bounded Rationality and Two-System Theory—Professional Skepticism 6
  - 1.4.1 Bounded Rationality 7
  - 1.4.2 Two-System Theory 8
  - 1.4.3 Linking Professional Skepticism to Bounded Rationality and Two-System Theory 9
- 1.5 A Summary of the Experiment. 10
- References. 11

2 Experimental Study. 13
- 2.1 About the Experimental Study 13
- 2.2 Abstract of the Study 14
- 2.3 Introduction 14
- 2.4 Key Concepts and Theory 17
  - 2.4.1 Professional Skepticism in the Auditing Standards 18
  - 2.4.2 Trait Versus Situational Professional Skepticism. 19
  - 2.4.3 Two-System Theory and Auditors' Skepticism 20
- 2.5 Conceptual Model and Hypotheses Development. 21
  - 2.5.1 Conceptual Model. 21
  - 2.5.2 Hypotheses 23
- 2.6 Method. 25
  - 2.6.1 Experimental Design. 25
  - 2.6.2 Participants 25
  - 2.6.3 Selection of the Study Sample 27
  - 2.6.4 Experimental Instrument 29

2.7 Results ... 31
2.7.1 Situational Professional Skepticism and Its Relationship to Manipulation Checks ... 32
2.7.2 Likelihood of a Valuation Problem ... 32
2.7.3 Evidence on Intuitive Auditors Versus Deliberate Auditors ... 35
2.8 Discussion ... 41
2.8.1 Conclusion ... 41
2.8.2 Two-System Theory and Professional Skepticism ... 42
2.8.3 Contribution to Practice ... 42
2.8.4 Future Research and Limitations ... 43
References ... 44

3 The Experimental Instrument ... 47
3.1 About the Experimental Instrument ... 47
3.2 The Experimental Instrument ... 49
3.2.1 The Audit ... 49
3.2.2 Inventory Business Process ... 51
3.2.3 Audit Task ... 52
3.2.4 Other Questions ... 52
3.2.5 Demographic Questions ... 54
Reference ... 54

Chapter 1
Auditors' Professional Skepticism

Abstract The International Standard on Auditing (IFAC, International Federation of Accountants (2009) in International Standard on Auditing 200 (ISA 200) Overall objectives of the independent auditor and the conduct of an audit in accordance with international standards on auditing. International Federation of Accountant (IFAC), NY, 2009, ISA No. 200) defines professional skepticism as a multifaceted mindset reflected in auditors' attitude. The professional skepticism multifaceted mindset is reflected in auditors' attitude and includes a questioning mind, alertness to circumstances that may imply misstatements due to error or fraud, and a critical evaluation of audit evidence (IFAC, International Federation of Accountants (2009) in International Standard on Auditing 200 (ISA 200) Overall objectives of the independent auditor and the conduct of an audit in accordance with international standards on auditing. International Federation of Accountant (IFAC), NY, 2009, ISA No. 200). In this chapter explains what professional skepticism is more in depth, why it is important to study professional skepticism and then discusses the challenges encountered by accounting researchers, professionals and regulators with respect to professional skepticism in accounting. Because an experimental study of professional skepticism is conducted in Norway, the chapter also presents the institutional settings in Norway. Finally, the chapter describes Two-System theory and affect which are used in the experimental study in the Chap. 2.

Keywords Accounting · Affect · International standard on auditing (ISA) · Challenges · Institutional settings in norway · Judgment and decision-making · Professional skepticism · Two-System theory

1.1 About the Book

Professional skepticism is defined in the International Standard on Auditing as "[a]n attitude that includes a questioning mind, being alert to conditions which may indicate possible misstatement due to error or fraud, and a critical assessment of audit evidence" (IFAC 2009, ISA No. 200.13.l.). This book take on the task of

C. Olsen, *A Study of Professional Skepticism*, SpringerBriefs in Accounting,
DOI 10.1007/978-3-319-49896-6_1

discussing the many challenges encountered by accounting researchers, professionals and regulators with respect to professional skepticism in accounting. The book is useful to accounting researchers, accounting students that wish to conduct an experiment in accounting and to professional auditors interested in judgment and decision research examining the issue of professional skepticism. Further, the book presents an experimental study (coauthored with Iris Stuart) to examine auditors' level of professional skepticism when varying risk information and affective information. Finally, the last chapter presents the full experimental instrument of the study in Chap. 2.

The next sections in this Chapter explain what professional skepticism is more in depth and why it is important to study professional skepticism. I discuss the problems encountered by auditors when exercising professional skepticism in an audit engagement. More specifically, I focus on the issue of the lack of professional skepticism among auditors that is motivating the experimental study in Chap. 2. Because we conduct the experimental study in Norway, I describe the institutional settings in Norway. Following that, I present the theoretical framework behind the study. In the final part of the section, I provide a summary of the experiment for those readers that are interested in an overview of the study and its results. In Chap. 2, those readers can also get a glance at the study by reading the short abstract in the beginning of Chap. 2.

Chapter 2 describes the experimental study (coauthored with Iris Stuart) and the reader can use the chapter outline as a roadmap for writing a classical article as follows. After the study abstract, a section introduces the experimental study. Next, the background section explains the studies the study key concepts and theories such as professional skepticism in the auditing standards, trait versus situational professional skepticism and Two-System theory. The background leads to the conceptual model and hypotheses development section. To test the hypotheses, we design an experiment with auditors as participants. The following section describes the selection of the study sample and the experimental instrument used in the study. The results indicate professional skepticism and its relationship to manipulation checks, the likelihood of a valuation problem, and evidence on intuitive auditors versus deliberate auditors. Finally, the chapter ends with a discussion section.

Chapter 3 displays the experimental instrument used in the study in Chap. 2. The instrument was used with auditors. As a student you may use the instrument in your own research. The experimental instrument asks the participants to act as auditors. The instrument consists of the experimental audit case regarding an inventory valuation problem. The full instrument can be administrated on paper as it is or online by implementing it on a survey software. The instrument may be adapted to other research purposes too.

Taken together, the book is relevant to accounting students and auditors and other readers in several ways. First, the book is relevant to accounting students because the book presents a roadmap for conducting an experiment. Specially, this is relevant when accounting students need to design an experiment for their master thesis, doctoral thesis or other assignments. In addition, they can adapt the instrument to their research question in order to use it and test their hypotheses.

For other audience, the book describes professional skepticism in the audit context with a summary of the experimental study in the end of Chapter 1 and in the abstract in the first section of Chap. 2.

1.2 Professional Skepticism

Professional skepticism is defined in the International Standard on Auditing as: "An attitude that includes a questioning mind, being alert to conditions which may indicate possible misstatement due to error or fraud, and a critical assessment of audit evidence" (IFAC 2009, ISA No. 200.13.l.). Being professionally skeptical in auditing is challenging because auditors find it difficult to apply the right level of professional skepticism. Professional skepticism (hereafter, PS) is required but regulators' inspections have revealed that auditors do not exercise enough PS in their audit judgments and decisions (IAASB 2012; PCAOB 2012). For instance, Jeanette M. Franzel, a board member at the PCAOB, has expressed the following:

> Academic research and PCAOB standards and oversight emphasize that professional skepticism is fundamental to the role and performance of auditors... Yet, the PCAOB and other regulators around the world have expressed concern about the continued high rate of audit deficiencies identified in their inspections and other oversight activities. And many of these deficiencies appear to be associated with the insufficient exercise of professional skepticism Franzel (2013) - Public Company Accounting Oversight Board (PCAOB) member.

In addition, academia sees PS as a "black box" (DeFond and Zhang 2014). The term, "black box," acknowledges the fact that nobody really knows how PS works. Moreover, PS is described as difficult to define (Nolder and Kadous 2014; Hurtt et al. 2013), and researchers are faced with conflicting perspectives on PS (Shaub 1996; Nelson 2009; Hurtt et al. 2013). Nolder and Kadous (2014) indicate that there is no single comprehensive measure of PS (Quadackers et al. 2014). Finally, researchers lack a precise theory that describes how PS works, and standard setters do not provide specific guidance on how to exercise or document PS.

In reaction to these problems both academia and standard setters have called for papers linking prior research findings around an accounting phenomenon such as PS (e.g. Kadous 2015; Nolder and Kadous 2014), for research on PS in general (e.g. Franzel 2013), for empirical research examining the role of affect in setting the level of PS (Hurtt et al. 2013). To respond to these calls we investigate with an experiment the role of affect and the role of personality characteristics in setting the level of professional skepticism and through a discussion of how neuroaccounting can penetrate the black box of professional skepticism.

In the study, we examine the following main research question: *How does PS (i.e. induced by client's risk) and interpersonal affect (i.e. auditors' intuitive affective reactions toward client's behavior) jointly influence auditors' skeptical judgments using a Two-System theory perspective*?

An adequate experimental instrument was developed to address the research questions of this thesis. Although the experimental instruments[1] used in the study is adapted from the experimental instruments of Bhattacharjee et al. (Bhattacharjee and Moreno 2002; Bhattacharjee et al. 2012) and Quadackers et al. (2009), it was necessary to adapt the instrument to the distinct research questions.

The instrument was pilot tested three times on fifty five (n = 55) participants of whom twenty-one (n = 21) were auditors, three accounting professors (n = 3) and the rest accounting students (n = 31) to ensure that the manipulation checks on affect and skepticism are appropriate. The auditors and the professors gave me additional feedback on the quality and the complexity of the task and the time allowed for the completion of the instrument. The instrument was modified accordingly to insure that the material was comprehensible, the task complexity was appropriate for accounting students and the time allowed was also appropriate. After these modifications, the instrument was administrated on auditors.

1.3 Institutional Settings in Norway

Because the study is done in Norway, we give in this section a brief overview of key facts on Norway, of the Norwegian social progress, culture and of the auditing profession in Norway.

Norway is a kingdom with a population 2014 over five millions, king Harald V is the king and Erna Solberg (from the Conservative Party) is the head of the Government. According to the World Bank,[2] Norway is a high income land with a Gross Domestic Product of GDP 2013 of $512.6 billion (current US$). The wealth in Norway comes from the massive oil and gas discovered in the 60s in the Norwegian Continental Shelf.[3] The surplus revenue is invested in the Government Pension Fund Global created in 1990 by the government in Norway in order to use it when the revenues in oil and gas phases down. By December 2014, the fund has accumulated over six billions Norwegian kroner.[4]

The United Nations (UN) measures different countries happiness (an emotion) in order to track social progress and inform the public policies in these countries. The likely reasons behind the countries levels are: GDP per Capita, years of healthy life expectancy, having someone to count on in times of trouble (e.g. social support),

[1]The background information on the ABC company in the instruments has been based on a real company; however all names and figures have been modified in order to keep the company anonymous.

[2]Downloaded December 4th, 2014. Available on: http://data.worldbank.org/country/norway.

[3]Downloaded December 4th, 2014. For more information visit: http://www.regjeringen.no/en/dep/oed/Subject/oil-and-gas/norways-oil-history-in-5-minutes.html?id=440538.

[4]Downloaded December 4th, 2014. Available on: http://www.nbim.no/.

perceptions of corruption, prevalence of generosity, and freedom to make life choices. The scores collected were than ranked from the happiest to the least happy country. Out of one hundred and fifty six surveyed countries, Norway is at the second place in the highest part of the rankings on happiness, while other countries such as the United States where at the seventeenth place and Singapore at the thirtieth place.[5] This suggests that Norwegian people are among the happiest countries in the world.

A description of the Norwegian culture is far from easy, however through Hofstede et al. (2010) model and online culture scores[6] it is possible to give a brief description of the Norwegian culture. The scores suggest that Norwegians have a relaxed attitude to hierarchies, societal classes and titles, they do not like controlling managers, and as employees they want to be consulted. Further on, Norway has a higher focus on the individual than on the group and the communication between Norwegians is direct. With respect to individual competitiveness and success, Norwegians do not appreciate individuals that brag or stand out of the crowd as a result of an individual achievement. This is commonly known as the law of Jante in Norway. Norwegians are seen as egalitarians (Cappelen et al. 2014). This means that Norwegians favor equality in social status in such way that people are seen as equal and treated equal (Arneson 2013).

With respect to the auditing profession in Norway, a *registered accountant* or a *certified public accountant* (CPA) must be approved by the Financial Supervisory Authority (FSA). These titles are granted when individuals fulfil three requirements in the Auditors Act[7] § § 3-2 to 3-3 and § 3-4. First, they have to accomplish a bachelor degree[8] in auditing to become a registered accountant or a master degree in accounting and auditing to become a CPA. Second, according to Auditors Act § 3-3, they have to complete three years of practical training in auditing financial statements. Third, they have to meet the requirements of good repute. In auditing the financial statements, auditors in Norway use the International Standards on Auditing (ISA).

The FSA also conducts the oversight of auditors. The FSA[9] is an independent body that is created through the laws and resolutions from the Norwegian Parliament, the Government, the Ministry of Finance and the international standards

[5]Downloaded December 4th, 2014. Available on: http://unsdsn.org/resources/publications/world-happiness-report-2013/.

[6]Downloaded December 2014. Available on: http://geert-hofstede.com/norway.html.

[7]The Auditors Act (OV-1999-01-15 2 Act on Auditing and Auditors) is available on: http://lovdata.no/dokument/NL/lov/1999-01-15-2#KAPITTEL_3 downloaded July 30, 2014.

[8]In Norway, higher education follows a 3 + 2 model, which refers to three years ending with a bachelor degree and then two years of education ending with a master degree.

[9]Information available on: http://www.finanstilsynet.no/no/Venstremeny/Om-Finanstilsynet/ downloaded July 30, 2014.

Table 1.1 Hand collected data from transparency reports available online (Audit firms that audit entities of public interest have to file transparency reports according to Auditors Act § § 5a-1 and 5a-2) for 2012–2013

Data on Audit firms in Norway	Year	Number of public entities	Revenues in million NOK	Assurance/audit and advisory	Tax	Consulting
EY	2013	141	2331	1241	393	697
PwC	2013	142	2307	1168	362	779
Deloitte	2013	70	1400	789	277	334
KPMG	2012	106	1199	751	184	264
BDO	2012	34	1076	801	127	148
RSM International	2012	2	122	77		45
Grant Thornton International	2012	3	45	23	2	20
Total			8480	4850	345	2287

for financial supervision. In general, the FSA in Norway aims to ensure financial stability and overall market conditions and that the users can rely on the financial agreements and services in the market. Since 2011, the Norwegian FSA has collaborated with the American Public Company Accounting Oversight Board (PCAOB) to conduct joint supervisions of audit firms registered in both the FSA and the PCAOB.

With respect to the audit market structure in Norway, Big 4 companies control the audit market. The table above reports Norwegian audit companies that audit entities of public interest in Norway in 2012–2013. Ernst & Young (EY) has the highest total revenues, followed by PricewaterhouseCooper (PwC), Deloitte and KPMG. The Big 4 companies in Norway represent about 85% of the revenues presented in the table. 57% of the audit firms' total revenues are revenues from audit and assurance services, and 43% of audit firms' revenues are from tax and consulting services (Table 1.1).

1.4 Bounded Rationality and Two-System Theory—Professional Skepticism

The theoretical framework in the study in Chap. 2 relies on the bounded rationality assumption and Two System theory. In this section, I discuss why the bounded rationality assumption, the Two System theory and that professional skepticism fits with the bounded rationality assumption and Two-System theory.

1.4.1 Bounded Rationality

Reasoning under the optimality principle claims the human adaptiveness is regarded as rational.[10] Determining optimality for rational behavior requires a quantifiable formulation of the problem, and the making of several key assumptions. When the goal or problem involves making a decision, rationality factors in how much information is available (e.g. complete or incomplete knowledge). Collectively, the formulation and background assumptions are the model within which rationality applies" available on: http://en.wikipedia.org/wiki/Rationality Economists assume that humans make decisions that maximize their utility (Simon 1979, as cited in; 1990) which is often called the normative discipline of decision theory. The normative decision theory answers questions such as how people should decide. The decision maker as a perfectly rational agent is supposed to act as a maximizer of expected value (Beach and Connolly 2005).

This perfectly rational agent assumption was never supported by experimental research (Campitelli and Gobet 2010). Simon (1955, 1956, 1957) criticized strongly the view of perfect rational agents. Simon pointed to factors that hinder a decision maker to act as perfectly rational agent. For instance, some of the factors that Simon listed are: the complexity of the environment, the non-availability of perfect and full information and the limited cognitive processing capacity of decision makers hinder decision makers to achieve rationality and maximization (Campitelli and Gobet 2010).

From a cognitive processing perspective, the decision maker (i.e., an auditor in this book) has a limited computing capacity and thereby a decision maker uses approximate methods to handle most tasks. Therefore, auditor's rationality is bounded (Simon 1990, 6) and he or she may choose to "satisfice" instead of maximization (Campitelli and Gobet 2010). "To satisfice is to choose a good enough option, not the best option" (Campitelli and Gobet 2010, 355).

Simon's three assumptions in decision-making are as following (Campitelli and Gobet 2010): (1) decision makers are not perfectly rational but rather bounded rational, (2) the quality of decisions vary in accordance with the level of expertise of an agent, and (3) the cognitive processes involved in decision making should be studied in order to study decision making. Thus, an investigation of only performance is not sufficient.

In the co-authored article, the assumption of bounded rationality is used because auditors' judgments and decisions are made with reasonable (i.e., approximate) amount of calculation, with incomplete amount of information and thus without an

---

[10]"In philosophy, rationality is the exercise of reason. It is the manner in which people derive conclusions when considering things deliberately. It also refers to the conformity of one's beliefs with one's reasons for belief, or with one's actions with one's reasons for action. However, the term "rationality" tends to be used in the specialized discussions of economics, sociology, psychology and political science. A rational decision is one that is not just reasoned, but is also optimal for achieving a goal or solving a problem. The term "rationality" is used differently in different disciplines.

exhaustive evaluation of all available options. Auditors as decision makers will probably choose to satisfy in their work and will act according to the bounded rationality assumption.

Kahneman and Tversky agreed with Simon that decision makers are not perfectly rational (Campitelli and Gobet 2010) and that the bounded rationality assumption will prevail in decision making. For instance, Kahneman developed the Two-System theory that is also based on the assumption that the human cognitive ability is limited and that conscious and unconscious processes may disrupt each other's. In Kahneman's Two-System theory, cognitive processes are called: System 1 and System 2. I describe the Two-system theory in the next section.

1.4.2 Two-System Theory

Two-System theory is part of the dual process theories and proposes two cognitive systems of reasoning operating in human decision-making (Sloman 1996; Stanovich and West 2000; Kahneman 2003, 2011). Stanovich et al. (2000), Kahneman (2003) labeled the two systems: System 1 and System 2. According to Kahneman (2003) System 1 operations are characterized as: "fast, automatic, effortless, associative, implicit (not available to introspection), and often emotionally charged; they are also governed by habit and are therefore difficult to control or modify" (Kahneman 2003, 698). System 2 operations are characterized as being "slower, serial, effortful, more likely to be consciously monitored and deliberately controlled; they are also relatively flexible and potentially rule governed" (Kahneman 2003, 698).

Moreover, System 2 is lazy (Kahneman 2011) or lax (Kahneman 2003). According to Kahneman the two system model suggests that System 1 is perceptual and generates intuitive operations such as impressions of perception and thought. Impressions are not voluntary and not explicit. Accordingly, System 1 is intuitive. System 2 monitors the mental operations and may disrupt the intuitive System 1. System 2 is deliberate in its processing, however, System 2 is lax and people, such as auditors, occupied with demanding tasks are more susceptible to allow intuitive System 1 judgment to be expressed because auditors tend to substitute a difficult question with an easier one. This indicates that System 2 has not modified the intuitive judgment.

Kahneman suggests that intuitive judgments can be both right or erroneous (Kahneman 2003). According to Sloman (1996), affect has a central role in intuitive System 1 judgment and in dual process theories (as two system theory in this paper) of thinking[11] in general. To understand how affect influence System 1, it is

[11]Damasio (1994) (Descartes' Error: Emotion, Reason, and the Human Brain) presented a theory based on observations of patients with damages to the ventromedial frontal cortices. The patients had intact intelligence, memory and logics but their ability to feel was impaired. These damages had destroyed the person ability to make rational decisions that is in his best interest. The ability to feel is to associate affect with the anticipated consequences of their actions. The brain damages resulted in a form of sociopathy (Damasio et al. 1990).

important to present Slovic et al. (2002) theoretical framework of how affect influence judgment and decision making in general. In Slovic et al. framework affect guides the judgment and decision making because affective responses happen automatically and rapidly and guide judgment and decision making in an unconscious way. For instance, stimulus words such as treasure and hate make people sense feelings and the reliance on such feelings in decision making is called affect heuristic[12] (Slovic et al. 2002).

Slovic et al. (2002) show that affective reactions may be used as an heuristic attribute in complex evaluations such as in evaluation of predicted performance of different industries. Kahneman and Frederick (2002) report that stimuli prompting affective evaluation occurs outside individuals' consciousness and affect heuristics are often used by decision makers' intuitive System 1 (Kahneman 2003). This may also happen in an audit setting. For instance, auditors' irrelevant interpersonal affective reactions toward the client may influence their evaluative judgments in an audit through an attribute substitution mechanism. More specifically, this indicates that auditors may use affect heuristic to do an evaluative judgment rather than relying on the deliberate System 2 resulting in an intuitive judgments. Thus, auditors' System 1 cognitive processing may result in an intuitive skeptical judgments and choices. Intuitive judgments and choices may be costly for the audit firm if they are erroneous.

1.4.3 Linking Professional Skepticism to Bounded Rationality and Two-System Theory

Auditors' are humans and according to Simon are bounded rational agents when they make judgments and decisions. Because professional skepticism is exhibited in auditors' judgment and decision making, auditors' level of professional skepticism is governed by the bounded rationality assumption. Relying on the bounded rationality assumption when applying professional skepticism means that there are limitations to how well auditors can do with respect to the exhibited level of professional skepticism in an audit. Remember that auditors may do several cognitive tasks; still, they have limited cognitive capacities.

When the auditors are bounded rational, auditors' cognitive processes that are used in their skeptical judgments and decisions may be explained by the Two-system theory. This means, auditors' use intuitive System 1 and deliberate System 2 cognitive processes to arrive to the appropriate level of professional skepticism exhibited in their skeptical judgments and decisions. Auditors' effortful

[12]Moreover, "it is proposed that people use an affect heuristic to make judgments; that is, representations of objects and events in people's minds are tagged to varying degrees with affect. In the process of making a judgment or decision, people consult or refer to an "affect pool" containing all the positive and negative tags consciously or unconsciously associated with the representations" (Slovic et al. 2002, 400).

cognitive processes (those that involve deliberate System 2) required by their tasks may disrupt (one task or another) while effortless cognitive processes (that involve intuitive System 1) may proceed with no disruption. This suggests that skeptical judgments may be of poor quality if they are based on the intuitive System 1 cognitive processes.

Prior literature in accounting finds that individuals having naturally a deliberate mindset (i.e., System 2) or interventions inducing the deliberate mindset increase the quality of judgment and decision making in accounting settings. For instance, Farrell et al. (2014) find that pay incentive that activates a deliberate mindset in accounting mangers have improved (but does not eliminate totally System 1 intuitive mindset) managers' investment choices. Griffith et al. (2015) indicate that interventions inducing deliberative mindset in auditors may increase audit quality. Therefore, hypotheses development on whether an intervention will improve auditors' skeptical judgments and decisions will include the cognitive process used by auditors while making the skeptical choice.

From that follows, the idea to use Two-System theory in the construction of the theoretical framework behind the experimental study presented in Chap. 2. The next section presents a summary of the experimental study in Chap. 2.

1.5 A Summary of the Experiment

Aims: The aims of the experiment is to examine (1) *whether*, (2) *how* professional skepticism (i.e. induced by client's risk) and interpersonal affect (i.e. auditors' intuitive affective reactions toward client's behavior) interact and influence auditors' skeptical judgments, and (3) to explore the effects of intuition, deliberation and gender on the auditor's skeptical judgment and skeptical decision.

Materials and methods: We use an audit questionnaire that we have developed based on a two (high risk versus low risk) by two (positive affect versus negative affect) experimental and between subject design.

Participants: Auditors.

Results: We find (1) that the influence of the affective information on the auditor's skeptical judgment will depend on the level of client risk in the audit engagement. Under high client risk, both positive and negative affective information on the client have made auditors more skeptical in their judgments. Under low client risk, positive affective information on the client has made auditors more skeptical in their judgments than negative affective information on the client. Further analysis suggests that affect heuristics has a subconscious influence on auditors' skeptical judgments in both intuitive and deliberate auditors, but the influence of affect is different. Interestingly, the presentation of positive client's behavior is leading deliberate auditors to be more skeptical in their judgments than when they are presented with negative clients' behavior while presentation of positive client's behavior leads intuitive auditors to be less skeptical in their judgments than when presented with negative clients' behavior. Differences in gender are associated with differences in skeptical judgment and skeptical choice.

Conclusions: Our findings support the Campitelli and Gobet (2010) view on including expertise as a refinement of Two-System theory. Professional skepticism is not only determined by cold cognition but also determined partly by auditors' *gut feelings* toward the client. Our evidence indicates that auditors' cognitive system (intuitive versus deliberate) moderates the influence of professional skepticism on skeptical judgments.

References

Arneson R (2013) Egalitarianism. In: Zalta EN (ed) The Stanford encyclopedia of philosophy. The Metaphysics Research Lab

Beach LR, Connolly T (2005) The psychology of decision making. People in organizations, 2nd edn. Sage Publications Series

Bhattacharjee S, Moreno K (2002) The impact of affective information on the professional judgments of more experienced and less experienced auditors. J Behav Decis Mak 15(4):361–377

Bhattacharjee S, Moreno K, Riley T (2012) The interplay of interpersonal affect and source reliability on auditors' inventory judgments. Contemp Account Res 29(4):1087–1108

Campitelli G, Gobet F (2010) Herbert Simon's decision-making approach: investigation of cognitive processes in experts. Rev Gen Psychol 14(4):354–364

Cappelen AW, Eichele T, Hugdahl K, Specht K, Sørensen EØ, Tungodden B (2014) Equity theory and fair inequality: a neuroeconomic study. Proceed Natl Acad Sci USA (PNAS) 111 (43):15368–15372

Damasio A (1994) Descartes' error: emotion, reason, and the human brain. G. P. Putnam's Sons, New York

Damasio AR, Tranel D, Damasio H (1990) Individuals with sociopathic behavior caused by frontal damage fail to respond autonomically to social stimuli. Behav Brain Res 41:81–94

DeFond M, Zhang J (2014) A review of archival auditing research. J Account Econ 58(2–3):275–326

Farrell AM, Goh JO, White BJ (2014) The effect of performance-based incentive contracts on System 1 and System 2 processing in affective decision contexts: fMRI and behavioral evidence. Account Rev 89(6):1979–2010

Franzel JM (2013) Auditor objectivity and skepticism—What's next? Anaheim. CA, American Accounting Association (AAA)—annual meeting

Griffith EE, Hammersley JS, Kadous K, Young D (2015) Auditor mindsets and audits of complex estimates. J Account Res 53(1):47–79

Hofstede G, Hofstede GJ, Minkov M (2010) Cultures and organizations: software for the mind 3rd edn. McGraw-Hill

Hurtt RK, Brown-Liburd HL, Earley CE, Krishnamoorthy G (2013) Research on auditor professional skepticism: literature synthesis and opportunities for future research. Auditing: A J Pract Theor 32(Supplement):45–97

IAASB (2012) International Accounting & Auditing Standards Board (IAASB) staff questions and answers: professional skepticism in an audit of financial statements. International Federation of Accountants (IFAC), New York

International Federation of Accountants (IFAC) (2009) International Standard on Auditing 200 (ISA 200). Overall objectives of the independent auditor and the conduct of an audit in accordance with international standards on auditing. International Federation of Accountant (IFAC), NY

Kadous K (2015) Panel on editors' views on issues in publishing research. American Accounting Association (AAA)—auditing section midyear meeting and doctoral consortium, Miami

Kahneman D (2003) A perspective on judgment and choice: mapping bounded rationality. Am Psychol 58(9):697–720

Kahneman D (2011) Thinking, fast and slow. Allen Lane, London

Kahneman D, Frederick S (2002) Representativeness revisited: attribute substitution in intuitive judgment. In: Gilovich T, Griffin D, Kahneman D (eds) Heuristics and biases. Cambridge University Press, New York

Nelson MW (2009) A model and literature review of professional skepticism in auditing. Auditing: J Pract Theor 28(2):1–34

Nolder C, Kadous K (2014) The way forward on professional skepticism: conceptualizing professional skepticism as an attitude. Suffolk University and Goizueta Business School at Emory University

PCAOB (2012) Public Company Accounting Oversight Board (PCAOB) Staff audit practice alert No. 10. Maintaining and applying professional skepticism in audits

Quadackers L (2009) A study of auditors' skeptical characteristics and their relationship to skeptical judgments and decisions. Vrije Universiteit, Amsterdam

Quadackers L, Groot T, Wright A (2014) Auditors' professional skepticism: neutrality versus presumptive doubt. Contemp Account Res 31(3):639–657

Shaub MK (1996) Trust and suspicion: the effects of situational and dispositional factors on auditors' trust of clients. Behav Res Acc 8:154–174

Simon HA (1955) A behavioral model of rational choice. Q J Econ 69(1):99–118

Simon HA (1956) Rational choice and the structure of the environment. Psychol Rev 63(2):129–138

Simon HA (1957) Models of man, social and rational. Oxford: Wiley

Simon HA (1979) The sciences of the artificial, 2nd edn. MIT Press, Cambridge

Simon HA (1990) Invariants of human-behavior. Annu Rev Psychol 41:1–19

Sloman SA (1996) The empirical case for two systems of reasoning. Psychol Bull 119(1):3–22

Slovic P, Finucane M, Petres E, MacGregor DG (2002) The affect heuristic. In: Gilovich T, Griffin D, Kahneman D (eds) Heuristics and biases. The psychology of intuitive judgment. Cambridge University Press, New York

Stanovich KE, West RF (2000) Individual differences in reasoning: Implications for the rationality debate? Behav Brain Sci 23(5):645–726

Chapter 2
Experimental Study

Abstract In this chapter follows the structure of a classical article in order to present an experimental study on auditors' professional skepticism. The title of the experimental study is "The Effects of Situational Professional Skepticism and Affect on Auditors' Skeptical Judgments: A Two-System Theory Perspective". This study is coauthored with Professor Iris, Stuart at the *Norwegian School of Economics*. In this study, professional skepticism is seen as a "black box" because the cognitive processes behind it are unknown. We experimentally investigate whether and how the interaction between professional skepticism and interpersonal affect influences auditors' skeptical judgments through a Two-System theory perspective. We use a two (high client risk versus low client risk) by two (positive versus negative affect) experimental design. We find a significant interaction between risk and affect. Our findings suggest that the influence of affective cues on auditors' skeptical judgments, will depend on the level of risk in the client engagement. Our study identifies affective reactions as important components of setting the level of professional skepticism and argues that the key in applying the right level of professional skepticism is in switching to the deliberate System 2 cognitive decision process under high risk conditions.

Keywords Affect · Article · Auditors · Deliberate cognitive process · Experiment · Interaction · Intuitive cognitive process · Professional skepticism · Risk

2.1 About the Experimental Study

The title of the experimental study is "The Effects of Situational Professional Skepticism and Affect on Auditors' Skeptical Judgments: A Two-System Theory Perspective". This study is coauthored with Professor Iris Stuart at the *Norwegian School of Economics*. The sections in this chapter follows the structure of a classical

C. Olsen, *A Study of Professional Skepticism*, SpringerBriefs in Accounting,
DOI 10.1007/978-3-319-49896-6_2

article. The next section will present the abstract of the article. Section 2.3 is the article introduction and guides the reader through the remaining sections as would an article do.

2.2 Abstract of the Study

Professional skepticism is still a "black box" because the cognitive processes behind it are unknown. We experimentally investigate whether and how the interaction between professional skepticism and interpersonal affect influences auditors' skeptical judgments through a Two-System theory perspective. System 1 is an automatic process that intuitive auditors use whereas System 2 is a deliberate process where auditors choose not to rely on their affective reactions. We use a two (high client risk versus low client risk) by two (positive versus negative affect) experimental design. We find a significant interaction between risk and affect. Our findings suggest that the influence of affective cues on auditors' skeptical judgments, will depend on the level of risk in the client engagement. When we examine how affective reactions influence the intuitive versus the deliberate auditors' skeptical judgments, we find that affective reactions are part of auditors' skeptical judgments regardless of whether auditors' use intuitive or deliberate processing, however the influence is different. The intuitive auditor seems to incorporate the affective cues into their skeptical judgments. The deliberate auditor consciously tries to avoid incorporating affect (reflected in their responses on the manipulation checks on affect) in their skeptical judgments reducing (but not eliminating) the influence of affect on their judgments. Our study identifies affective reactions as important components of setting the level of professional skepticism and argues that the key in applying the right level of professional skepticism is in switching to the deliberate System 2 cognitive decision process under high risk conditions.

2.3 Introduction

Even as professional skepticism[1] is important to regulators (IAASB 2012; PCAOB 2012, 2013), to audit quality (Knechel et al. 2012; Glover and Prawitt 2013) and to auditing research on auditors' judgments (e.g. Kadous et al. 2013), so also are hard-wired[2] emotions (affect) important to human judgment and decision making

---

[1]In International Standards on Auditing (ISA) professional skepticism is defined as "[a]n attitude that includes a questioning mind, being alert to conditions which may indicate possible misstatement due to error or fraud, and a critical assessment of audit evidence" (IFAC 2009, 77).

[2]Hard-wired describes the fact that emotions, feelings and affective reactions toward objects, subjects or in decision-making will occur in humans intuitively such in the case of affect heuristics (Kahneman 2011).

(Tversky and Kahneman 1981; Damasio 1994; Shaub 1996; Kahneman 2003, 2011) and to skeptical judgment and behavior (Hurtt et al. 2013; Nolder and Kadous 2014). Thus, hard-wired affect may influence the level of professional skepticism exhibited by the auditors. Yet an understanding of professional skepticism and its impact on auditor's judgments is still a "black box"[3] (DeFond and Zhang 2014, 4), and research on the role of affect in accounting settings is limited (Kida et al. 2001; Moreno et al. 2002; Bonner 2008; Hurtt et al. 2013).

Our study addresses this gap in the literature by examining *whether* and *how* professional skepticism (induced by client risk) and interpersonal affect (auditors' intuitive affective reactions toward client's behavior) interact and influence auditors' skeptical judgments. We use the Two-System theory, to evaluate auditors' skeptical judgments.

Researchers in accounting and standard setters disagree on whether affective reactions toward the client are to be seen as non-diagnostic[4] information on client's behavior that influences auditors' judgments. We cannot address this issue in depth in our paper, for it can be a topic of research in its own right. We will, however, briefly identify the main issues behind these conflicting views. In one stream of research, scholars argue that non-diagnostic interpersonal affect is a priori irrelevant and does not influence auditors' skeptical judgments (Hackenbrack 1992; Bhattacharjee et al. 2012). This stream of research describes the influence of affect heuristics[5] on judgment as biasing auditors' judgments. We give participants the type of affective information about client's behavior that these accounting researchers predict should bias auditors' skeptical judgments if used in the decision process. By contrast with this facet of research, standard setters seem to recommend that auditors use their *gut feeling* in establishing the right level of professional skepticism in their judgments. For instance, SAS No. 99 (AICPA 2002, AU §316.68) suggests that client's behavior and the interpersonal relationship between the auditor and the client's management should influence auditors' professional skepticism. This issue of whether client's behavior should influence auditors' judgments remains unresolved.

Moreover, we only address *situational* factors elicited by the client's risk and behavior but not *trait* factors. Although trait professional skepticism is important, Shaub (1996) indicates that situational factors are prevalent in setting the level of

---

[3]Despite the importance of professional skepticism, it is described as a black box (DeFond and Zhang 2014). We use the term of black box here because nobody really knows what professional skepticism is. For instance, professional skepticism is ill-defined (Hurtt et al. 2013), researchers are faced with conflicting perspectives on professional skepticism (Shaub 1996; Nelson 2009; Hurtt et al. 2013), there is no single comprehensive measure of it (Quadackers 2009), and we lack a precise theory that explains professional skepticism.

[4]Non-diagnostic information refers to information that is not useful for making a judgment or a choice.

[5]The decision maker uses affect heuristics as a short-cut when he uses affect as an important cue in the decision process instead of engaging in effortful search for information involving the deliberative reasoning system (Kunda 1999; Slovic et al. 2002; Kahneman 2011).

professional skepticism. A second advantage of using situational factors instead of trait skepticism is the possibility of changing these factors in order to enhance the level of professional skepticism that is the objective of many standard setters (e.g. IAASB 2012).

Our first situational factor is situational professional skepticism that is induced by client risk (Quadackers et al. 2014). We expect that framing risk at two levels (low and high) will trigger different levels of professional skepticism in an auditor's judgment. Our second situational factor is interpersonal affect. Interpersonal affect refers to the auditor's intuitive and heuristic affective reactions toward the client's behavior. We do not call it non-diagnostic or irrelevant as has been done in the prior literature (Bhattacharjee et al. 2012) because our focus is not to test the relevancy of the client's behavior but rather our focus is to understand the processes behind setting the level of professional skepticism.

As we are addressing the influence of intuitive affect heuristics on auditors' skeptical judgments, we think that the Two-System theory distinctions between intuitive (unconscious) System 1 and deliberative System 2 (Kunda 1999; Kahneman 2011) can describe/illuminate the role of affect in auditors' skeptical judgments. This is because auditors have been shown to use heuristics as rules of thumb in their judgments (Pike et al. 2013; Kadous et al. 2013). Two-System theory has also added insights in how the affect heuristic influences managers' decisions (Farrell et al. 2014).

Using a two (high risk versus low risk) by two (positive affect versus negative affect) between subject design with auditors, we examine the influence of situational professional skepticism (through client risk) and interpersonal affect (through affective information on client's behavior) on auditors' skeptical judgments. In addition, we ask auditors to justify their skeptical judgments with a memo explanation to avoid the *dilution effect*[6] and to insure that the results have real world implications (Hackenbrack 1992).

Consistent with our predictions, we find a significant interaction between risk and affect that influences the auditor's skeptical judgment. This means that the influence of the affective information on the auditor's skeptical judgment will depend on the level of client risk in the audit engagement. We find that under high client risk, both positive and negative affective information on the client have made auditors more skeptical in their judgments. The fact that positive affective

[6]Hackenbrack (1992) argues that experiments that only look to the effects of non-diagnostic evidence with diagnostic evidence have a narrow focus because the experimental results are not producible in real worlds. The dilution effect refers to the fact that participants' judgments will be less extreme when non-diagnostic evidence is mixed with diagnostic evidence. Thus, the lab results are often a result of the dilution effect where non-diagnostic evidence dilutes the effects of diagnostic evidence. The magnitude of this effect is dependent on whether the non-diagnostic information is able to attract the participant's attention. He recommends that experiments ask participants to justify their judgments or use decision aids, as this is often the case in a real world environment, to avoid the hypothetical dilution effect and insure that experimental results have real world implications.

information has increased auditor's skeptical judgment under high risk could not be predicted by the Two-System theory. Under low client risk, positive affective information on the client has made auditors significantly more skeptical in their judgments than negative affective information on the client.

Our further analysis of the results to investigate how the interaction takes place suggests that affect has a subconscious influence on auditors' skeptical judgments in both intuitive and deliberate auditors; however, the influence of affect is different. Interestingly, the positive client's behavior makes deliberate auditors more skeptical in their judgments than when they are presented with negative clients' behavior while positive client's behavior made intuitive auditors less skeptical in their judgments than negative client's behavior. We also report that differences in gender are associated with differences in skeptical judgment.

Our findings contribute empirically to research on professional skepticism (Hurtt et al. 2013; Quadackers et al. 2014; Nolder and Kadous 2014) and affect in accounting settings (Bhattacharjee and Moreno 2002; Bhattacharjee et al. 2012; Guénin-Paracini et al. 2014). This contribution has two aspects. First, our empirical contribution differs from the research approach of prior literature (Bhattacharjee et al. 2012; Quadacker et al. 2014) because we bring in two levels of client risk (i.e. high risk and low risk), which have not been investigated in prior studies in the presence of affective information. We believe this an important addition to prior research as it emulates the audit environment reality where auditors are exposed both to different levels of risk and to different types of affective information on clients' behavior.

Second, our finding that auditors become skeptical in the presence of positive affective information under high client risk is important. As mentioned before, the direction of this result could not be predicted based on the Two-System theory. We explain this result as an expression of auditors' expert knowledge of professional skepticism gained through education and audit experience. In other words, expert knowledge of professional skepticism has an impact on how affect influences auditors' judgments. This result supports prior suggestions to include expertise in the Two-System model (Campitelli and Gobet 2010).

We structure the remainder of this paper as follows. The next section gives a review of key concepts and theory underlying the study. Section 2.3 describes our conceptual model and the derived hypotheses. Section 2.4 describes the method. In Sect. 2.5, we present our results. Section 2.6 reports the conclusions and the implications of our study.

2.4 Key Concepts and Theory

In this section, we review relevant literature on professional skepticism and affect, and we explain Kahneman's Two-System theory.

2.4.1 Professional Skepticism in the Auditing Standards

The International Auditing and Assurance Standards Board (IAASB) of the International Federation of Accountants (IFAC) and the Public Company Accounting Oversight Board (PCAOB) explain professional skepticism in similar ways.

> Professional skepticism—An attitude that includes a questioning mind, being alert to conditions which may indicate possible misstatement due to error or fraud, and a critical assessment of audit evidence (IFAC 2009, ISA No. 200.13.l.)… The auditor shall plan and perform an audit with professional skepticism recognizing that circumstances may exist that cause the financial statements to be materially misstated (IFAC 2009, ISA No. 200.A15)… The auditor shall exercise professional judgment in planning and performing an audit of financial statements (IFAC 2009, ISA No. 200.16).

> The PCAOB standards define professional skepticism as an attitude that includes a questioning mind and a critical assessment of audit evidence. The standards also state that professional skepticism should be exercised throughout the audit process… When auditors do not appropriately apply professional skepticism, they may not obtain sufficient appropriate evidence to support their opinions or may not identify or address situations in which the financial statements are materially misstated (PCAOB 2012, 1).

These descriptions of professional skepticism suggest that the auditor should have the ability to recognize situations or factors that require either more or less professional skepticism in judgment and decision-making. This means that auditors should deliberately adjust their level of professional skepticism to the situation at hand. Accordingly, auditors employ the level of professional skepticism that is required in order to identify and address circumstances that may cause the financial statements to be materially misstated. For instance, auditors find it necessary to determine whether a given circumstance constitutes either a high or a low risk of material misstatements. Situations where the risk of material misstatement is high will require a higher level of professional skepticism than situations where the risk of material misstatement is low. This distinction and the appropriate response should be exercised throughout the audit process.

The consequences of failing to use an adequate level of professional skepticism (PCAOB 2012) may cause the auditor to gather less audit evidence than is appropriate to the circumstance and thereby fail to control audit risk to an acceptable level. Accordingly, it is problematic when auditors fail to apply sufficient professional skepticism because audit quality will suffer. As a response to this problem, standard setters (IAASB 2012) and researchers (Glover and Prawitt 2013, 2014) have called for *enhancing* professional skepticism. We understand enhancing professional skepticism as exercising higher levels of skepticism. Exhibiting higher levels of skeptical judgment is for instance judging that the likelihood of a valuation problem in an audit engagement is very probable. This means that auditors have a presumptive doubt or are suspicious that something can go wrong in the financial statements.

2.4.2 Trait Versus Situational Professional Skepticism

Although accounting researchers have defined professional skepticism and sought to understand it in various ways, its precise nature and influence on auditor judgment in specific circumstances is still a black box (DeFond and Zhang 2014); the concept is ill-defined (Hurtt et al. 2013; Nolder and Kadous 2014), and there is no single comprehensive measure of it (Quadackers 2009). Indeed, existing research does not yet demonstrate a consistent unified perspective or approach for exploring this topic. Recent studies have examined professional skepticism from a variety of methods. For instance, research has explored professional skepticism directly through conceptual modeling (Nelson 2009; Hurtt et al. 2013; Nolder and Kadous 2014), by using trust and suspicion toward the client as a proxy for professional skepticism (Shaub 1996), or qualitatively by considering the complexity of the audit task (Griffith et al. 2014), by examining the individual ability such as "IQ, cognitive reflection, numeracy" (Kadous 2012, 3) of the auditor, by measuring skepticism as a trait (Hurtt 2010) or experimentally as a consequence of the client's risk on auditors' judgments (Nelson 2009; Quadackers et al. 2014).

In general, researchers agree that professional skepticism is reflected in the auditors' skeptical judgments and actions (e.g. Hurtt et al. 2013; Kadous et al. 2013; Nolder and Kadous 2014) and is determined by dispositional (such as a trait) and situational factors (Shaub 1996; Hurtt 2010). For instance, Shaub (1996) describes professional skepticism as an attitude reflective of suspicion. Griffith et al. (2014) look to auditors' overreliance on management numbers when faced with an audit of complex estimates, while Hurtt and colleagues (Hurtt 2010; Hurtt et al. 2013) see professional skepticism as a combination of trait[7] and state professional skepticism.

We do not address trait skepticism in this study but rather focus on situational professional skepticism. In this experiment, we use client risk as a proxy for situational skepticism to elicit skeptical behavior. One reason for only addressing situational factors in this paper is that we lack a precise measure for trait skepticism (Quadackers 2009). Another reason is that prior research (Shaub 1996) reported that situational skepticism is more prevalent than trait skepticism in setting the level of professional skepticism. A third reason is the emphasis scholars have given to the attitudinal rather than trait factors in the conceptualization of professional skepticism (Nolder and Kadous 2014).

[7]Trait skepticism is the term used to describe "a relatively stable and enduring aspect of an individual" (Hurtt 2010, 150). By contrast, state skepticism is a "temporary condition aroused by situational variables" (Hurtt 2010, 150).

2.4.3 Two-System Theory and Auditors' Skepticism

Kahneman's Two-System theory (Kahneman 2003) is the *overarching* theory in this study because it seems to describe the unknown mechanism behind setting the level of professional skepticism in auditors' skeptical judgments. We choose the Two-System theory because prior research reports that it was successful in explaining judgment and decision-making biases and how to mitigate these biases (e.g. Kahneman 2011). Therefore, given the lack of a formal theory on professional skepticism, we believe that this theoretical construct will increase our understanding of what happens when auditors make skeptical judgments, and the use of this theory offers solutions to improve the quality of auditors' skeptical judgments.

Kahneman proposes that two cognitive systems of reasoning operate in human judgment and decision-making (Kahneman 2003, 2011). The two systems are the intuitive/heuristic System 1 and the deliberative/analytical System 2 (Stanovich and West 2000; Kahneman 2003). System 1 reasoning occurs without conscious thought and is present as a baseline System in the human brain (Farrell et al. 2014), while System 2 reasoning requires more effort on the part of the decision maker. System 2 reasoning requires a deliberate action on the part of the decision maker to activate.

Prior research has identified a tension in the Two-System theory regarding the quality of judgment and decision-making when heuristics (also called rules of thumb or mental shortcuts) are used. The intuitive judgment based on the affect heuristic can be either right or wrong, but most importantly, it occurs unconsciously (Kahneman 2003). Consequently, at times the judgment made by the auditor using System 1 thinking does result in a correct judgment, but often the judgment is incorrect because System 1 reasoning does not use relevant evidence (Bhattacharjee et al. 2012) in making judgments and decisions.

The expert knowledge of an auditor may express *professional skepticism* as an automatic reaction to *client risk*, an intuitive, "System 1" function. For instance, we know that other professionals, including chess players and physicians, use their intuition on a daily basis to decide effectively and their intuitive "leaps" often lead to sound decisions (Kahneman 2011). This habitual usage may explain why experts' intuition often leads to right answers.

Whether *interpersonal affect* is relevant or irrelevant to auditors' decision process is subject to conflicting views in the auditing literature. Some researchers assume non-diagnostic interpersonal affect is irrelevant and should not influence auditors' skeptical judgments (Bhattacharjee et al. 2012). Accordingly, the client's characteristics and behavior should not determine decision making within an audit. Yet, Bhattacharjee and Moreno (2002) find that evaluations of *irrelevant* client characteristics made by less experienced auditors (i.e., whether they are inclined to like client management) do have an influence on these auditors' judgments. Robertson (2010) also finds that clients' behavior has an influence on auditors' judgments. Clients ingratiating the auditor (i.e., a client trying to induce positive affect in the auditor to influence the auditor's judgment in favor of the client's request) influence auditors' judgments only when the client has a low incentive to try to influence the auditor. This stream of research describes the influence of affect heuristics on judgment as biasing auditors' judgments. In this study, we give participants the type of affective cues that these accounting researchers predict should bias auditors' skeptical judgments and should lead them to the wrong decision if used in their decision-making.

Another group of researchers do not address affect at all; several merely conclude it is important to the auditor's judgment or decision and then comment that auditing research is limited on the role of affect (e.g. Bonner 2008). By contrast, a third view point in accounting research suggests that client's behavior and characteristics may be indicative of poor client integrity and may signal whether a client tries to manipulate the financial numbers. For instance, Ball (2009) suggests that management's nonfinancial motives can often reveal whether a client will commit a fraud. This viewpoint and evidence suggest that auditors should be alert to client's behavior and be wary of behavior that may be intended to manipulate. In this context, affective reactions toward the client behavior will be good for auditors' professional skepticism.

In another aspect of the current scene, regulators and standard setters require auditors to take into account client's behavior in the audit of financial statements. For instance, SAS No. 99 (AICPA 2002, AU §316.68) suggests that client's behavior and the interpersonal relationship between the auditor and client's management will influence auditors' professional skepticism. AU §316.68 enumerates circumstances arising from the relationship between the auditor and the client which require higher levels of professional skepticism in the assessment of risk such as when the client intimidates the auditor, causes delays in the audit work or denies the auditor access to evidence.[8]

In this study, the tension is that we do not know whether auditors will use a deliberate decision making model in their skeptical judgments or stick to their baseline intuition (Farrell et al. 2014). Auditors have not been taught to control affective information and engage in deliberative reasoning when they make a skeptical judgment about the likelihood of a valuation problem. This may lead them to make an intuitive judgment that occurs automatically based on whether they like or dislike the client.

2.5 Conceptual Model and Hypotheses Development

2.5.1 Conceptual Model

We now introduce our conceptual model in Fig. 2.1 based on the theory developed in the previous section. We test in our hypotheses whether the auditor's skeptical

[8]See section 316 *Consideration of Fraud in a Financial Statement Audit* paragraph 68 *Assessing risks of material misstatement due to fraud throughout the audit,* under *Problematic or unusual relationships between the auditor and management.*

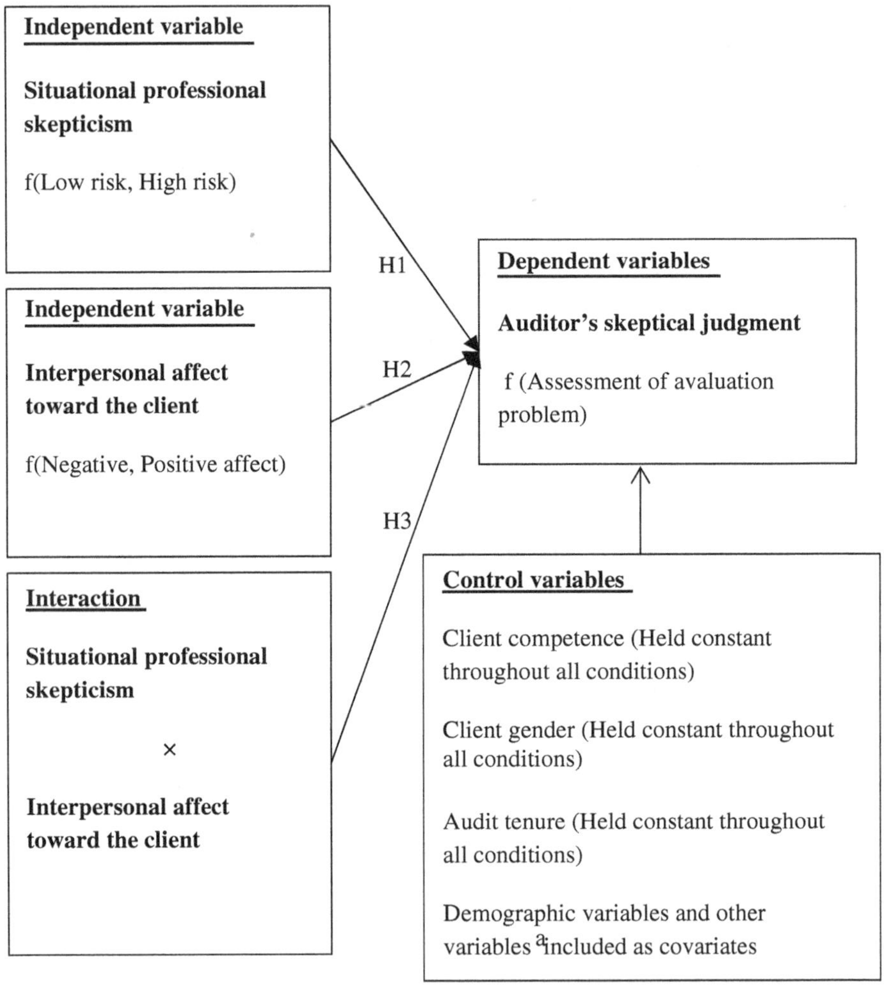

Fig. 2.1 Conceptual model and variable definition. *Notes* [a]Demographic variables and other variables include: gender, firm, rank, audit experience, inventory experience, and mode of case completion (online or paper copy)

judgment is a function of both the auditor's interpersonal affect toward the client and the level of situational professional skepticism in the case. Control variables include client competence, the auditor's work experience in auditing, and various demographic characteristics of the client or auditor. We hold client competence and audit tenure constant throughout all conditions.

According to Two-System theory, affect will influence auditors' judgments if the auditors act as intuitive decision makers. This is due to the intuitive processing mechanism in human decision-making. If auditors, by contrast, act as deliberate decision makers, their skeptical judgments will be more reflective of the risk in the audit engagement.

2.5.2 *Hypotheses*

We test whether situational professional skepticism (risk) and interpersonal affect (affect) influence the auditors' skeptical judgments. Prior evidence on the impact of the risk of material misstatements on auditors' judgments is mixed. For instance, auditors are found to be more skeptical when the risk in an audit engagement is high (Quadackers et al. 2014). By contrast, regulatory inspections of the PCAOB (2013) report that in engagements with a high risk of material misstatements, auditors do not respond to risk and do not express enough professional skepticism. In addition, little is known about how auditors' responses to different risk levels will influence their skeptical judgments. Consequently, the effect of situational professional skepticism on auditors' skeptical judgments is unclear. Hypothesis 1 tests the main effect of situational professional skepticism on auditors' judgments. In the various conditions associated with this experiment, auditors are expected to exhibit more skeptical judgment when client risk is high than when it is low.

HYPOTHESIS 1. *Under high risk, auditors will assess an inventory valuation problem to be more likely than when risk is low.*

Two-System theory posits that if auditors act as intuitive decision makers their skeptical judgments will reflect the intuitive assessment of whether they like or dislike the audit client. If auditors act as deliberate decision makers, they will override the effects of affective information about the client behavior by engaging in the deliberate processing of System 2. Deliberate processing will result in a skeptical judgment more reflective of client's riskiness than the client's behavior. Based on the Bhattacharjee et al. (2012) findings on negative affect and the fact that affective reactions are hard-wired in human decision-making (Damasio 1994), we expect negative affect to influence auditors if they act as intuitive decision makers.

We do not know whether and how positive affective information about the client will influence auditors' skeptical judgments. We also do not know whether auditors use deliberate decision-making or intuitive decision-making. It is possible that auditors use deliberate thinking and avoid making decisions based on affect because of the requirement of being professionally skeptical. It is also possible that auditors use intuitive thinking and include affective information in their judgments because the affective reaction to the client is hard-wired in the auditor. Thus, it is unclear whether auditors will incorporate affective reactions in their skeptical judgments. Therefore, hypothesis 2 tests the overall main effect of affect on auditors' skeptical judgments.

HYPOTHESIS 2. *Affective information about client's behavior will influence auditor's assessment of the likelihood of an inventory valuation problem.*

Both situational professional skepticism and interpersonal affect are present in the audit setting. The interaction between professional skepticism and affect has not been investigated in prior literature (Hurtt et al. 2013). Although Bhattacharjee et al. (2002, 2012) find that negative affective information on the client influences auditors' risk assessments, neither Bhattacharjee et al. (2012) nor other studies have investigated the relation between positive affect and professional skepticism. Consequently, we want to test in our hypothesis whether the interaction occurs, but we will not predict the direction of how the interaction happens because it is unknown.

Figure 2.2 depicts the influence of positive affect as a *fan* because the slope of the influence can point upwards or downwards (Elliott et al. 2013). According to Elliott et al. (2013), such a depiction reflects the fact that we do not have an a priori theory or empirical findings to do directional predictions of the influence of positive affect on skeptical judgments in the presence of high risk or low client risk. From that follows Hypothesis 3 below, which tests the interaction between risk and affect.

HYPOTHESIS 3. *Interpersonal affect and situational professional skepticism will interact such that auditors faced with differing levels of risk will judge the likelihood of the inventory obsolescence problem differently when faced with negative affective information about the client than when faced with positive affective information about the client.*

Two-System theory describes that decision makers using their intuitive System 1 may arrive at a different judgment than decision makers using their deliberate System 2 (e.g. Farrell et al. 2014). In our study, intuitive auditors' skeptical judgments will reflect the affective cues given in the case while deliberate auditors' skeptical judgments will be more reflective of client's risk. The Griffith et al. (2015) study suggests that inducing a deliberative mindset helps auditors make higher

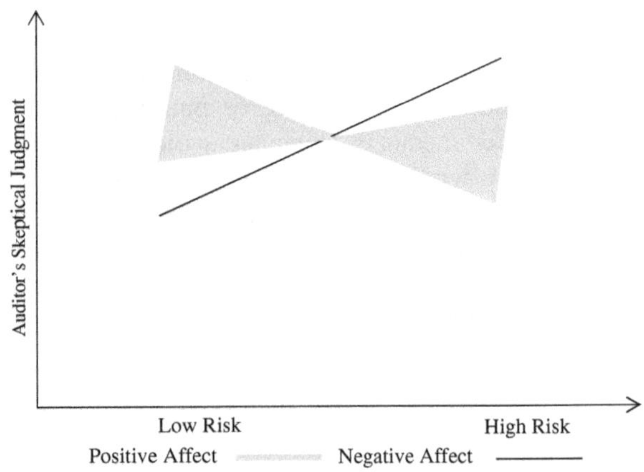

Fig. 2.2 A depiction of the hypothesized interaction between risk and affect. *Notes* We know little about how positive affect influences skeptical judgment and therefore we draw our prediction as a fan (Elliott et al. 2013)

quality decisions in the audit of complex estimates than auditors in other mindsets (Griffith et al. 2015). They do not, however, address professional skepticism in their study. In our setting, we predict that there will be differences between the skeptical judgments of intuitive auditors compared to deliberate auditors, but we do not know how the direction or extent of the differences. This is because there is no prior literature that addresses the comparison of deliberate and intuitive auditors with respect to their professional skepticism. From this context comes the following non-directional hypothesis:

HYPOTHESIS 4. *Auditors' skeptical judgments regarding the likelihood of an inventory obsolescence problem will vary between auditors using intuitive and deliberate decision making strategies.*

2.6 Method

2.6.1 Experimental Design

The experimental design used in this study is a two by two design resulting in four experimental conditions. We manipulate situational professional skepticism on two levels: high risk and low risk. Then, we manipulate interpersonal affect on two levels: positive affect and negative affect.

Demographic variables (gender, firm, rank, audit experience, inventory experience, and online) were included as covariates, and in the data analysis we find only gender to be significant to auditors' skeptical judgments. We hold constant audit tenure (five years), client's competence (highly competent) and client's gender (male) throughout the conditions.

We randomize the effects of auditors' traits across the conditions because we randomly assigned the auditors to the four conditions.

2.6.2 Participants

In our study, we solicited participants with audit experience between 1 and 5 years by contacting the following sources in Norway: the Big 4 audit firms, two audit firms that are not Big 4 and the Norwegian Institute of Public Accountants (hereafter, DnR). Table 2.1 reports information about the participants from each source. All audit firms provided participants except one Big 4 audit firm that did not respond to our request for participants.

In Table 2.1, we provide information on how the data was gathered at each source, including online collection (random assignment of the conditions through Qualtrics) and paper collection (conditions assigned in random order). One Big 4

Table 2.1 Source, environmental controls and participants

Source	Environmental controls			Participants				
Firm	Moderator	Arrangement	Paper or online	Number available	N = 190 6 conditions	N = 128 4 conditions	N = 59 final	Rates[g]
Firm 1 Big 4 Office 1[a]	Firm	Training session	Paper	45	30	19	7	67%
Firm 1 Big 4 Office 2[a]	Firm	Training session	Paper	25–35	15	8	4	50%
Firm 2 Big 4	First author and partner	Training session	Paper	60	60	45	22	100%
Firm 3 Big 4	Link to auditors	Training session	Online	49	37	27	17	76%
DnR[b] conferance	First author	Session	Paper	108[c]	27	17	6	25%
Firm 1 non Big 4	Link passed on to auditors	Online	Online	NA[d]	15	9	3	NA
Firm 4 Big 4[e]	NA	NA	NA	NA	NA	NA	NA	NA
Firm 2 non Big 4[f]	Link passed on to auditors	Online	Online	100	6	3	0	6%
Sum					190	128	59	

[a]Firm 1 is a big 4 firm provided participants from two offices in two different locations in Norway (office 1 and office 2). The firm contact informed us that the number of participants approached in one of the offices was between 25 and 35 participants in the training session. Further we use the average number 30 in calculating the participation rates

[b]DnR is a Norwegian abbreviation for The Norwegian Institute of Public Accountants. DnR arranges a yearly conference for their members. The first author distributed the questionnaires on paper in random order to participants in one of the conference sessions

[c]The number of members participating in the conference session. The DnR contact notified us that this number included not only auditors but may include other types of professionals too (e.g., lawyers)

[d]We do not have the number of how many were initially approached to take the study online for firm 1 non Big 4

[e]One Big 4 firm did not give us access to their auditors

[f]The partner in this firm estimated that he sent the link to 100 other partners in this firm

[g]Based on the number of auditors approached (available) and the initial collected sample (N = 190), participants average participation rate for the on paper administration is 61% (= (0.67 + 0.5 + 1 + 0.25) × 100%/4) and the online administration is 41% (= (0.76 + 0.06) × 100%/2)

firm and the DnR allowed the first author to administer the instrument in their training sessions. The other audit firms administrated the questionnaires themselves either in their training sessions or online by passing on the link to their auditors.

In accordance with the ethical research requirements in Norway, we informed all the auditors that their participation in the study was on a volunteer basis. Based on the number of auditors approached and the initial sample collected of one hundred and ninety (N = 190) participants, the average rate for the paper administration is 61% (= (0.67 + 0.5 + 1 + 0.25) × 100%/4) and for the online administration is 41% (= (0.76 + 0.06) × 100%)/2). Note that on Table 2.1, we do not have the number of how many participants were approached initially to take the study online for firm 1 non Big 4.

We collected data from 190 participants in six experimental conditions and selected a participant sample of 59 as follows. The results from four experimental conditions are discussed in this paper (128 participants), while the two other experimental conditions (with only the skepticism manipulation and no interpersonal affect manipulation) will not be discussed in this paper or in another paper. We dropped these two conditions because we discovered that these two conditions were not realistic in the audit context. Then, we applied manipulation checks to the data from 128 participants that resulted in a participant sample of 59 discussed below in more detail.

2.6.3 *Selection of the Study Sample*

Only the participants[9] who answered the manipulation checks correctly were included in our study because our objective is to contribute with (1) new empirical knowledge on the interaction between professional skepticism and affect and (2) an improved understanding about the Two-System processes behind professional skepticism. In this context, we eliminate the participants who do not pay attention to our manipulations.

Our manipulation checks on skepticism asked the auditor's professional skepticism to report their opinion on whether the client's controller has a strong motivation to manipulate short term results on a scale from 1 = Strongly disagree to 7 = Strongly agree. We had four manipulation checks on affect. The first manipulation check item asked auditors to report their opinion on whether they like the client's controller on a scale from 1 = Strongly disagree to 7 = Strongly agree. The second manipulation check asked the participants to report their opinion on whether

[9]One hundred and twenty-eight auditors participated in the study. We dropped 12 participants who did not complete the questionnaire and 57 did not pass the manipulation checks on both affect and on skepticism. We limited our sample to 59 auditors who passed the manipulation checks because we want to understand those auditors who are sensitive to environmental changes. Of these 59 auditors, 20 completed the questionnaires online and 39 completed the questionnaires on paper as shown in Table 2.2.

they are frustrated with the client's controller on a scale from 1 = Strongly disagree to 7 = Strongly agree. The third manipulation check item asked the participants to report their opinion on whether they are happy with the client's controller on a scale from 1 = Strongly disagree to 7 = Strongly agree. Finally the fourth manipulation check asked the participants to report their opinion on they are irritated with the client's controller on a scale from 1 = Strongly disagree to 7 = Strongly agree.

For our sample in Table 2.2, we require auditors to have the correct answers on the skepticism item because we induce two levels of situational professional skepticism. We drop the respondents who answer the skepticism question incorrectly. Second, we require auditors to respond correctly to at least three of the four manipulation checks on affect. The final sample includes a mixture of both intuitive and deliberative auditors who have passed both the skepticism and interpersonal affect manipulations.

Table 2.2 Descriptive statistics of the selected sample

Demographics	N = 59
Gender	
Male	30
Female	29
Firm type	
One of the Big 4 firms	50
An international audit firm that is not a Big 4 firm	3
A national audit firm	2
Other	4
Rank	
Staff auditor	8
Senior/associate senior auditor	46
Manager auditor	1
Partner auditor	3
Other	1
Audit experience	
Under 1 year	5
1–3 years	41
4–5 years	5
More than 5 years	8
Inventory experience	
No experience	18
Deal with a number of occasions	37
Deal with very often	4
Online	
Online	20
On paper	39

As shown in Table 2.2, the sample consists of 59 auditors, 30 males and 29 females. 50 auditors were from Big 4 audit firms, while eight auditors were from other firms and one auditor worked in a central tax office. With respect to the auditors' ranks: eight were staff auditors, 46 were senior auditors, one was a manager, three were partners and one was a tax auditor.[10] All participants have audit experience.

2.6.4 Experimental Instrument

As shown in Fig. 2.3, the experimental instrument consisted of two parts. In part 1, the auditors received information on the study and the instructions on completion. Then, we provided them with the experimental audit case that described ABC, a hypothetical company that sells designer maternity clothing to small specialty clothing shops.

We provided the auditors with background information about the client, information regarding the relevant accounting standard for inventory valuation, a set of prior year audited financial statements and current-year unaudited financial statements, and ratios for both the prior year and the current year. At ABC, the controller is responsible for accounting for inventory. He has a law degree and an accounting degree and has served in several positions in ABC. We describe him as highly competent. This information is held constant across all four conditions. After auditors have read the background information about the company, we tell the auditors either that the risk of material misstatement for the valuation assertion of inventory is low or that it is high. Participants received the following information depending on their risk condition:

> The audit partner believes that the risk of material misstatement is *low* for the valuation assertion of inventory. The controller will revalue inventory at year-end if economic or industry conditions indicate that the company may not be able to sell inventory at a sales price equal to its cost. The controller does not receive a bonus based on an increase in net income, so he has no reason to avoid revaluing inventory to net realizable value if needed.
>
> *OR*
>
> The audit partner believes that the risk of material misstatement is *high* for the valuation assertion of ABC's inventory. The controller does not like to write down inventory even if economic or industry conditions indicate that the company may not be able to sell inventory at a sales price equal to its cost. The controller receives a bonus if net income increases by 13%. In the past, he has used the estimate of inventory obsolescence to make sure that net income increases by the amount needed so he gets his bonus.

[10]The participant had more than 5 years audit experience and therefore is kept here in the sample.

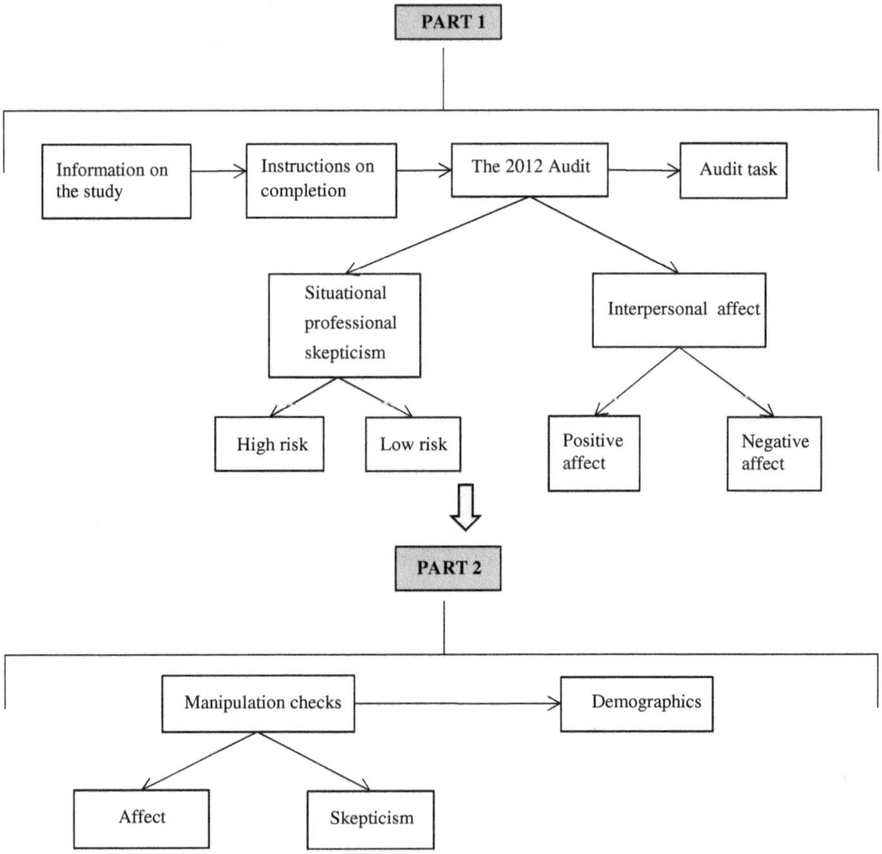

Fig. 2.3 The flow of the experimental instrument

Then participants in the positive or negative affect condition randomly received one of the following instructions from the audit partner on the engagement:

> ABC's success has made the controller very arrogant and difficult to deal with. Last year, Mike Jenkins, one of our seniors, wanted to meet with the controller to get some information on the inventory system. The controller has a good reputation in the industry and really knows what he is doing. But he refuses to work with the audit staff. Last year the controller refused to meet the audit senior, saying that he was too busy. It was not as if the controller was trying to hide anything. I had several meetings with him during this time, and he was always very cooperative. He just did not want to take the time to talk to someone at a lower level in the audit firm.
>
> *OR*
>
> The company has been very successful and the controller is easy to work with. Last year, Mike Jenkins, one of our audit seniors, wanted to meet with the controller to get some

> information on their inventory system. The controller has a good reputation in the industry and really knows what he is doing. He was happy to explain the system to Mike Jenkins. The controller repeatedly met Mike saying that he was always available whenever he needed to speak with him. I also had several meetings with the controller during this time and he was always very cooperative.

The affect vignettes induce auditors' affective reactions by giving auditors positive or negative information about the controller's personal characteristics. With this information, we evoke auditors' liking or disliking of the client.

The next section of the case provides information relevant to the inventory business process and the likelihood of writing inventory down to net realizable value because it is lower than cost:

> ABC is facing a new global competitor OHO who established a low price maternity clothing brand in mid-2011. According to OHO's press release in December 2011, OHO advertised an average selling price of $40 per item. This is lower than ABC's average selling price of $50 per item. ABC believes that it may have either to reduce its selling price to $40 in 2013 or compete with OHO by advertising a higher quality product. The controller has not written the inventory down because the company has not made the final decision about which of the two alternatives to follow.

The information about the inventory business process gives contradictory cues in such a way that the judgment in the audit task is not intrinsically clear to participants with regard to whether there is a valuation problem. The intention is to give some room for the manipulations of interpersonal affect and for situational professional skepticism to function and create variations. Although some would argue that the inventory valuation problem is very likely, auditors know that the client would prefer not to write down the inventory because a write down will influence company profitability. This makes the judgment unclear and therefore has an impact on auditors' ratings of the valuation problem.

After reading the information, auditors evaluate the likelihood that the client may have a valuation problem on a scale from 1 to 7, where 1 = Very unlikely and 7 = Very likely (Appendix 1). This judgment measures the effect of interpersonal affect and situational professional skepticism on auditors' skeptical judgments. Finally, the auditors received part 2 of the instrument where they are asked to answer the manipulation check questions and the demographic questions.

2.7 Results

In this section, we report the results on our manipulation checks, four hypotheses on auditors' skeptical judgments and the results of our further analysis.

2.7.1 Situational Professional Skepticism and Its Relationship to Manipulation Checks

In our experimental instrument, we measure auditors' situational professional skepticism (hereafter, skepticism) as the ability to be suspicious of management intentions. Auditors are asked to rate whether the client's controller has a strong motivation to manipulate short-term results on a scale from 1 = Strongly disagree to 7 = Strongly agree.

Table 2.3 panel A reports a correlation matrix between the different manipulation check items and the dependent variable skeptical judgment in this study. The risk manipulation is highly correlated with our item on situational professional skepticism item (r = 0.96). The next highest correlation is between skepticism and the item measuring auditors' irritation (r = 0.53).

We run an ANOVA to test our manipulation of client risk and our measurement of skepticism. We see that the risk manipulation is highly associated (p-value = 0.00) with the auditors' situational professional skepticism. Thus, variations in client risk are associated with variations in auditors' situational professional skepticism. As shown in panel B, our proxy client risk significantly explained over 90% of the variation in auditors' skepticism. Gender is marginally significant p-value = 0.09 for predicting auditors' situational professional skepticism.

2.7.2 Likelihood of a Valuation Problem

Table 2.4 panel A presents the descriptive statistics of the mean of auditors' skeptical judgments on the likelihood that the client has a valuation problem (1 = Very unlikely to 7 = Very likely). Under the low risk condition, auditors judge the likelihood of a valuation problem as more likely under the positive affect condition (mean = 5.47) than under the negative affect condition (mean = 4.25). Under the high risk condition auditors' skeptical judgments show that auditors judge the likelihood of a valuation problem as very likely under both the positive condition (mean = 5.67) and the negative affect condition (mean = 5.56).

Table 2.4 panel B shows the ANOVA analysis of variance for the main and the two-way interaction effects. In order to investigate how interpersonal affect (affect) and situational professional skepticism (risk) influence auditors' judgments, the ANOVA results are based on auditors' judgments on the likelihood that the client has a valuation problem (1 = Very unlikely to 7 = Very likely). As shown in panel B, Hypothesis 1 is supported because the main effect of risk is significant at a 5% level (p-value = 0.02).

Throughout the conditions auditors' assessment of the likelihood of an inventory valuation problem is significantly different and higher (mean = 5.60) when risk is high than when it is low (mean = 4.97). Hypothesis 2 is also supported because the

Table 2.3 Correlation matrix between the manipulation checks and the dependent variables and testing client risk as a proxy of situational professional skepticism

Panel A: correlation matrix between the manipulation checks and the dependent variables

	Skepticism	Skeptical judg.	Risk	Affect	Like	Frustrated	Happy	Irritated
Skepticism[a]	1.00							
Skeptical judg.[b]	0.29	1.00						
	(0.03)							
Risk[c]	0.96	0.27	1.00					
	(0.00)	(0.04)						
Affect[d]	0.14	−0.22	0.19	1.00				
	(0.28)	(0.09)	(0.16)					
Like[e]	−0.34	0.14	−0.34	−0.76	1.00			
	(0.01)	(0.30)	(0.01)	(0.00)				
Frustrated[f]	0.37	−0.07	0.34	0.74	−0.87	1.00		
	(0.00)	(0.61)	(0.01)	(0.00)	0.00			
Happy[g]	−0.43	0.04	−0.40	−0.72	0.84	−0.89	1.00	
	(0.00)	(0.77)	(0.00)	(0.00)	(0.00)	(0.00)		
Irritated[h]	0.53	0.03	0.48	0.67	−0.80	0.87	−0.81	1.00
	(0.00)	(0.80)	(0.00)	(0.00)	(0.00)	(0.00)	(0.00)	

Panel B: testing client risk as a proxy of situational professional skepticism

Source	Partial SS	Df	MS	F	Prob > F
Model	244.67	2	122.33	338.27	0.00
Risk	239.09	1	239.09	661.11	0.00
Gender[i]	1.08	1	1.08	2.98	0.09
Residual	20.25	56	0.36		
Total	264.92				
N	59				
R-squared	0.92				
Root MSE	0.60				
Adj R-squared	0.92				

Notes

The *p*-values are stated in parentheses

[a]Skepticism = Manipulation check of the auditor's situational professional skepticism measured by the auditors' assessment of whether the controller has a strong motivation to manipulate short-term results on a scale from 1 = Strongly disagree to 7 = Strongly agree

[b]Skeptical judg. = The outcome variable for skeptical judgment

[c]Risk = This variable presents the client risk manipulation in the case

[d]Affect = This variable represents the manipulation of interpersonal affect in the case

[e]Like = Manipulation check for whether auditors like the client's controller on a scale from 1 = Strongly disagree to 7 = Strongly agree

[f]Frustrated = Manipulation check for whether auditors are frustrated with the client's controller on a scale from 1 = Strongly disagree to 7 = Strongly agree

[g]Happy = Manipulation check for whether auditors are happy with the client's controller on a scale from 1 = Strongly disagree to 7 = Strongly agree

[h]Irritated = Manipulation check for whether auditors are irritated with the client's controller on a scale from 1 = Strongly disagree to 7 = Strongly agree

[i]Gender is measured by a categorical variable for gender coded as male = 1 and female = 2

Table 2.4 Auditors' skeptical judgments of the likelihood of a valuation problem

Panel A: descriptive statistics, number of observations (N), mean (standard deviation)

Conditions	Positive affect	Negative affect	Total
Low risk	N = 17	N = 12	N = 29
Mean	5.47	4.25	4.97
SD	(0.80)	(1.60)	(1.32)
High risk	N = 12	N = 18	N = 30
Mean	5.67	5.56	5.60
SD	(1.07)	(0.98)	(1.00)
Total	N = 29	N = 30	N = 59
Mean	5.55	5.03	5.29
SD	(0.91)	(1.40)	(1.20)

Panel B: analysis of variance

Source	Partial SS	Df	MS	F	Prob > F	H
Model	23.81	4	5.95	5.33	0.00	
Risk	6.55	1	6.55	5.86	0.02	H1
Affect	5.40	1	5.40	4.83	0.03	H2
Risk × affect	4.55	1	4.55	4.07	0.05	H3
Gender	7.31	1	7.31	6.55	0.01	
Residual	60.29	54	1.11			
Total	84.10	58	1.45			
N	59					
R-squared	0.28					
Root MSE	1.06					
Adj R-squared	0.23					

Panel C: tests of simple effects

Source	Df	F	Prob > F
Negative affect versus positive affect given low risk	1	8.80	0.01
Negative affect versus positive affect given high risk	1	0.02	0.90

Notes
Risk = high or low risk of material misstatement in the valuation assertion for inventory
Affect = positive or negative
Skeptical judgment = likelihood of valuation problem
Gender = male or female
All other covariates (firm, rank, audit experience, inventory experience, and method of administrating the questionnaire) were not significant

analysis of variance shows significant main effect for affect (p-value = 0.03) indicating that in all conditions affect influences auditors' ratings of the inventory obsolescence problem.

Hypothesis 3 tests whether there is an interaction effect between interpersonal affect and situational professional skepticism and it is significant at the 5% level (p-value = 0.05) in our two-way ANOVA and the interaction is ordinal. We also find that differences in auditors' gender are significantly (p-value = 0.01) associated with differences in auditors' skeptical judgments. The direction of this result is in

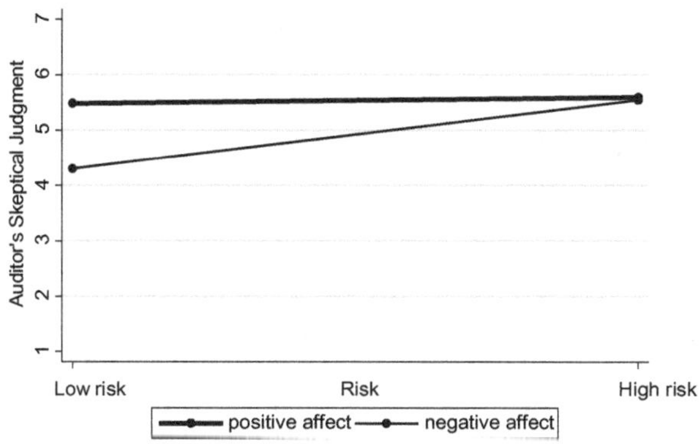

Fig. 2.4 ANOVA Plot—The interaction of risk × affect. *Notes* Auditors' skeptical judgments of the likelihood of a valuation problem in client's inventory on a scale 1 to 7 where 1 = Very unlikely, 2 = Unlikely, 3 = Somewhat Unlikely, 4 = Undecided, 5 = Somewhat Likely, 6 = Likely and 7 = Very likely

such way that female auditors are associated with higher levels of skeptical judgments (mean = 5.69) than male auditors (mean = 4.90).

Follow up tests for the interaction effect between risk and affect are reported in panel C of Table 2.4. We find significant differences in auditors' skeptical judgments of the likelihood of a valuation problem under the low risk condition but not under the high risk condition. Indeed only under the low risk condition, we find that auditors' skeptical judgments under the positive affect condition are significantly (p-value = 0.01) different than auditors' skeptical judgments under the negative affect condition.

As depicted in Fig. 2.4 with an ANOVA plot the influence of affect on auditors' judgments depends on the level of client risk in the audit engagement. The ANOVA plot shows an ordinal interaction (see Buckless and Ravenscroft 1990) between the two variables. As seen in Fig. 2.4, under low risk, auditors become more skeptical when positive affective information is present than when negative information is present. Under high risk, Fig. 2.4 shows that auditors get skeptical under both the positive and the negative affective conditions.

2.7.3 *Evidence on Intuitive Auditors Versus Deliberate Auditors*

In our mixed sample we can identify the intuitive and the deliberate auditors based on how the auditors answered the manipulation checks on affect. The variable *intuitive* designates with 1 the intuitive auditors and with 0 the deliberate auditors. We run a full factorial three-way ANOVA (risk × affect × intuitive) on the influence of situational professional skepticism (risk), interpersonal affect (affect) and intuition (System 1) on auditors' judgments of the likelihood of a valuation problem in client's inventory on a scale 1 = Very unlikely to 7 = Very likely.

Table 2.5 reports a significant interaction effect between two variables: *intuitive* and *affect*. In model (1), we include gender and audit experience. Gender is included because it is significant and audit experience is included to eliminate alternative explanations and show it is not significant. Model (2) controls for gender because it is a significant covariate and excludes audit experience as it not a significant covariate. The results suggest that the influence of interpersonal affect on skeptical judgments depend on whether the auditor uses the intuitive System 1 or has engaged the deliberate System 2.

In Table 2.6, we run a two-way ANOVA on the intuitive subsample of auditors (n = 40). In Table 2.5 panel A, we report that under low risk, intuitive auditors' skeptical judgments of the likelihood of a valuation problem are higher under positive affect (mean = 5.50) than under negative affect (mean = 4.40). The contrary result is observed under high risk where auditors' skeptical judgments of the likelihood of a valuation problem are higher under the negative affect condition (mean = 5.85) than under the positive affect condition (mean = 5.00). The results in panel B, report a significant interaction effect (p-value = 0.01) between risk and affect in the intuitive group.

The ANOVA plot in Fig. 2.5 depicts this interaction effect for the intuitive subsample. As seen below, the interaction is a disordinal (crossover) interaction that eliminates the significant main effects of risk and affect.

In Table 2.7 we report the results of the same two-way ANOVA for the deliberate subsample of auditors (n = 19). In panel A below, we see that under low risk, deliberate auditors' skeptical judgments of the likelihood of a valuation problem are higher under positive affect (mean = 5.33) than under negative affect (mean = 3.50). The same result is observed under high risk where deliberate auditors' skeptical judgments of the likelihood of a valuation problem are higher under the positive affect condition (mean = 5.89) than under the negative affect condition (mean = 4.80).

As reported in the analysis in panel B, we do not find a significant interaction between risk and affect. However, we find a significant main effect as shown below in Table 2.6 of affect (p-value = 0.03) on the deliberate auditors' skeptical judgments. Thus, even those deliberate auditors who view that affective cues are irrelevant through our manipulation checks have used the intuitive decision model because we see a significant main effect of affect.

The ANOVA plot below shows the absence of the interaction effect between risk and affect on deliberate auditors' skeptical judgments.

The ANOVA slopes in Figs. 2.5 and 2.6 provide support hypothesis 4 that intuitive and deliberate auditors have different skeptical judgments as we can see that the slope of intuitive (interaction) in Fig. 2.5 and the slope of deliberate auditors (no interaction) in Fig. 2.6 are different from one another.

Table 2.5 Three-way ANOVA between variables risk, affect and intuitive

Model	(1)					(2)					
Source	Partial SS	Df	MS	F	Prob > F	Partial SS	Df	MS	F	Prob > F	H
Model	33.82	11	3.07	2.87	0.01	29.58	8	3.70	3.39	0.00	
Risk	5.58	1	5.58	5.21	0.03	3.91	1	3.91	3.58	0.06	H1
Affect	2.75	1	2.75	2.57	0.12	5.03	1	5.03	4.61	0.04	H2
Risk × affect	3.80	1	3.80	3.55	0.07	5.17	1	5.17	4.74	0.03	H3
Intuitive[a]	0.34	1	0.34	0.31	0.58	0.40	1	0.40	0.37	0.55	
Risk × intuitive	1.13	1	1.13	1.05	0.31	0.84	1	0.84	0.77	0.38	
Affect × intuitive	2.13	1	2.13	1.99	0.17	4.05	1	4.05	3.71	0.06	
Risk × affect × intuitive	1.40	1	1.40	1.31	0.26	0.39	1	0.39	0.36	0.55	
Gender	3.94	1	3.94	3.68	0.06	5.95	1	5.95	5.43	0.02	
Audit experience[b]	4.24	3	1.41	1.32	0.28						
Residual	50.28	47	1.07			54.52	50	1.09			
Total	84.10	58	1.45			84.10	58	1.45			
N	59					59					
R-squared	0.40					0.35					
Root MSE	1.03					1.04					
Adj R-squared	0.26					0.25					

Notes

[a]Intuitive = Intuitive is a categorical variable coded as follows: intuitive = 1, deliberate = 0

[b]Audit experience = This demographic categorical variable measures how many years of experience auditors have with the following categories: None = 1, under 1 year = 2, 1–3 years = 3, 4–5 years = 4, and More than 5 years = 5

Table 2.6 Intuitive auditors' skeptical judgments of the likelihood of a valuation problem

Panel A: descriptive statistics, number of observations (N), mean (standard deviation)

Conditions	Positive affect	Negative affect	Total
Low risk	N = 14	N = 10	N = 24
Mean	5.50	4.40	5.04
SD	(0.85)	(1.58)	(1.30)
High risk	N = 3	N = 13	N = 16
Mean	5.00	5.85	5.69
SD	(1.00)	(0.80)	(0.87)
Total	N = 17	N = 23	N = 40
Mean	5.41	5.22	5.30
SD	(0.87)	(1.38)	(1.18)

Panel B: analysis of variance

Source	Partial SS	Df	MS	F	Prob > F	H
Model	23.45	4	5.86	6.63	0.00	
Risk	0.50	1	0.50	0.56	0.46	H1
Affect	0.02	1	0.02	0.02	0.90	H2
Risk × affect	6.17	1	6.17	6.98	0.01	H3
Gender	10.64	1	10.64	12.04	0.00	
Residual	30.95	35	0.88			
Total	54.4	39	1.39			
N	40					
R-squared	0.43					
Root MSE	0.94					
Adj R-squared	0.37					

Notes

We split the sample in two subsamples: intuitive auditors and deliberate auditors according to how they responded to the manipulation check items. We run a full factorial two-way ANOVA (risk × affect) with the sample containing only intuitive auditors. Except for gender all the other covariates were not significant

Fig. 2.5 ANOVA plot—The interaction of risk × affect for only the intuitive auditors

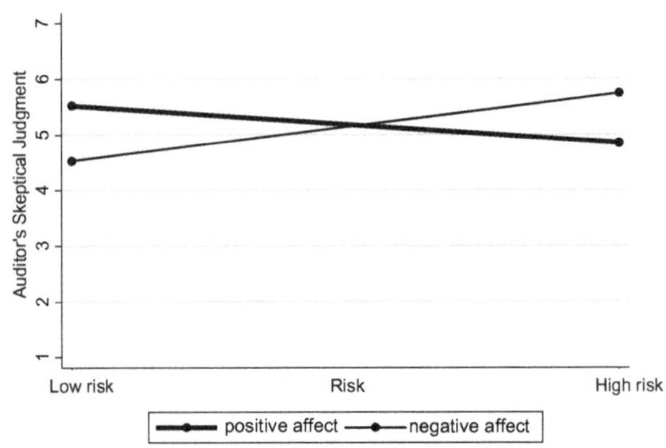

Table 2.7 Deliberate auditors' skeptical judgments of the likelihood of a valuation problem

Panel A: descriptive statistics, number of observations (N), mean (standard deviation)			
Conditions	Positive affect	Negative affect	Total
Low risk	N = 3	N = 2	N = 5
Mean	5.33	3.50	4.60
SD	(0.58)	(2.12)	(1.52)
High risk	N = 9	N = 5	N = 14
Mean	5.89	4.80	5.50
SD	(1.05)	(1.10)	(1.16)
Total	N = 12	N = 7	N = 19
Mean	5.75	4.43	5.26
SD	(0.97)	(1.40)	(1.28)

Panel B: analysis of variance						
Source	Partial SS	Df	MS	F	Prob > F	H
Model	10.34	2	5.17	4.28	0.03	
Risk	2.63	1	2.63	2.17	0.16	H1
Affect	7.36	1	7.36	6.09	0.03	H2
Residual	19.34	16	1.21			
Total	29.68	18	1.65			
N	19					
R-squared	0.35					
Root MSE	0.94					
Adj R-squared	0.37					

Notes

We use only the sub-sample on deliberate auditors. We run a full factorial two-way ANOVA (risk × affect) with the sample containing only deliberate auditors. The covariates were also tested and excluded because they were not significant

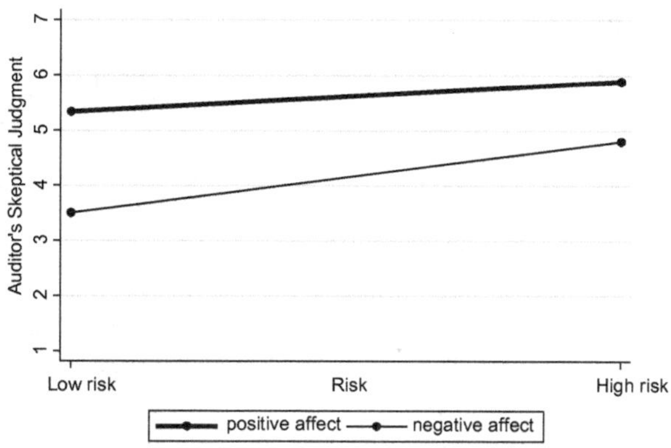

Fig. 2.6 ANOVA plot—The interaction of risk × affect with only the deliberate auditors

Table 2.8 Comparison of the results of the intuitive auditors versus the deliberate auditors

Panel A: the ANOVA plots of the interaction of risk × affect in intuitive auditors versus deliberate auditors

Intuitive auditors

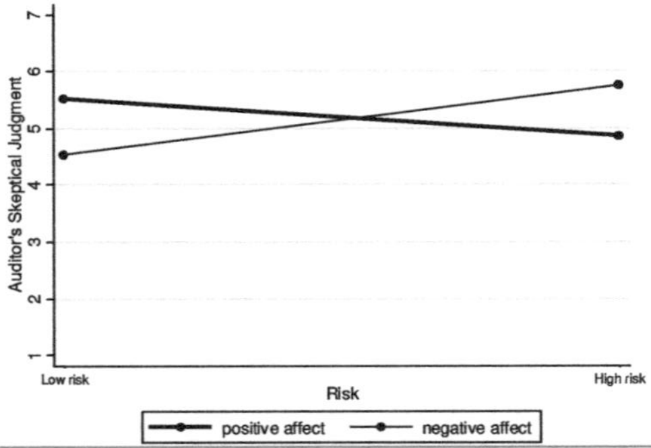

Deliberate auditors

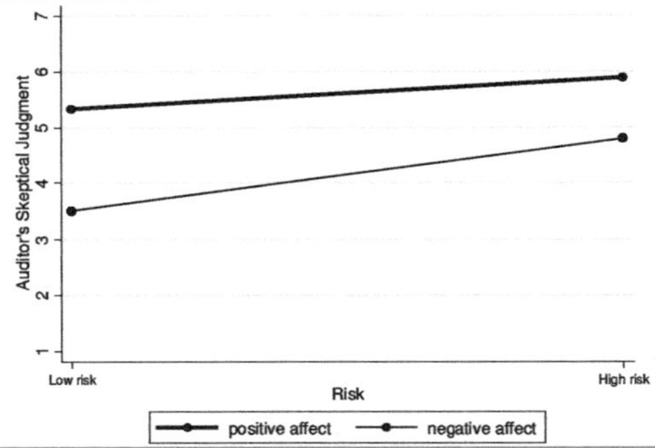

Panel B: comparison of the descriptive statistics, number of observations (N), mean (standard deviation) of intuitive versus deliberate auditors

	Intuitive auditors			Deliberate auditors		
Conditions	Positive affect	Negative affect	Total	Positive affect	Negative affect	Total
Low risk	N = 14	N = 10	N = 24	N = 3	N = 2	N = 5
Mean	5.50	4.40	5.04	5.33	3.50	4.60
SD	(0.85)	(1.58)	(1.30)	(0.58)	(2.12)	(1.52)
High risk	N = 3	N = 13	N = 16	N = 9	N = 5	N = 14
Mean	5.00	5.85	5.69	5.89	4.80	5.50
SD	(1.00)	(0.80)	(0.87)	(1.05)	(1.10)	(1.16)
Total	N = 17	N = 23	N = 40	N = 12	N = 7	N = 19
Mean	5.41	5.22	5.30	5.75	4.43	5.26
SD	(0.87)	(1.38)	(1.18)	(0.97)	(1.40)	(1.28)

2.8 Discussion

2.8.1 Conclusion

Our study has two objectives. The first objective is to investigate *whether* an interaction effect exists between situational professional skepticism and interpersonal affect on auditors' skeptical judgments. We find a significant interaction effect of risk and affect on auditors' skeptical judgments.

We report that under low risk, auditors become more skeptical when positive affective information is present than when negative information is present. The influence of affective information on auditors' skeptical judgments is different in the high risk condition. Indeed under high risk, auditors become skeptical with both the positive and negative affective information. Accordingly, auditors will have an enhanced level of professional skepticism if the risk of material misstatement is framed as high and the influence of other information (whether it is positive or negative affective information) will only make them more skeptical under a high risk situation. Our analysis also reports that differences in gender are associated with differences in skeptical judgments where female auditors exhibit higher levels of skeptical judgments than male auditors.

The second objective in this paper is to investigate how the interaction takes place based on the rationale of Two-System theory. We find that auditors are influenced by affect heuristics even though they have said in the manipulation check questions that they will not consider their affective reactions to the client's behavior under the manipulation checks on affect. Our results suggest that affect influence auditors' skeptical judgments regardless of whether they use intuitive or deliberate decision-making. The type of influence, however, is different. To better understand why this happens, we compare the results of the two groups.

In Table 2.8, we compare the results of skeptical judgments of the intuitive auditors versus the results of skeptical judgments of deliberate auditors. In panel A the ANOVA plots show that in the case of the intuitive auditors, affect heuristics have unintended effects on auditors' skeptical judgments because a disordinal interaction indicates that the influence of affect has one kind of influence on one level of risk; while the affect has the opposite influence under the other level of risk. In the case of deliberate auditors the interaction is absent indicating that the affect has the same influence regardless of the level of risk. The plots show that the difference is in the high risk condition.

In Table 2.8 panel B, we see that under the condition of high risk and positive affective reactions toward the client the intuitive auditors have on average judged the high risk lower (mean = 5.00) than the deliberate auditors (mean = 5.89). Under the condition of high risk and negative affective reactions toward the client, the result is the contrary and the difference is even bigger. The intuitive auditors' skeptical judgments are on average higher (mean = 5.85) than the deliberate auditors' skeptical judgments (mean = 4.80).

2.8.2 Two-System Theory and Professional Skepticism

We use a general psychological theory (i.e. Two-System theory) to develop the hypotheses in an expert setting. This means that this study considers the role of expertise in Kahneman's Two-System model. Remember: Two-System theory is a general story about an intuitive System 1 and a deliberative System 2 that have been used on naïve subjects with no consideration of professional knowledge (Campitelli and Gobet 2010). Accordingly, this study is different from a psychology study that uses the Two-System theory without addressing professional knowledge. To the best of our knowledge, no prior study considers Two-System theory on auditors' skeptical judgments as we do in this study. Our findings support the Campitelli and Gobet (2010) view on including expert knowledge as a refinement of Two-System theory because expert knowledge may influence intuitive and deliberate experts to behave differently than intuitive and deliberate non-experts.

Second the findings in this paper suggest that professional skepticism is not only determined by cold cognition but also determined partly by auditors' *gut feelings* toward the client as suggested in SAS No. 99. Our evidence indicates that auditors' cognitive systems (intuitive versus deliberate) moderate the influence of professional skepticism on skeptical judgments. For instance, in the deliberate auditor's skeptical judgment is influenced by the processing of hard-wired negative affective reactions toward a client. Interestingly, positive affective cues about the client made the deliberate auditors' subconsciously highly skeptical regardless of the level of professional skepticism exercised.

2.8.3 Contribution to Practice

Our overall results show that once the client risk is framed as high (for instance by an audit partner), the additional information in the audit client environment that is usually present will exacerbate the level of subsequent professional skepticism applied in the right direction. Because of this, it is possible to *enhance* professional skepticism in audit settings by framing the risk of material misstatement in an audit engagement as high. This would be good news for practice and for standard setters because it may well be that no costly training is needed to enhance professional skepticism.

However, the additional evidence suggests that it is not enough that auditors recognize the different types of cues in an audit of a client to arrive at the right level of skeptical judgment. Auditors need to be taught when and how to use their deliberate processing under high risk conditions.

The finding on gender effects is important. First, it is important in terms of its implications for practice. For instance, it offers a simple and a practical way for practitioners to enhance professional skepticism through appropriate gender mix in audit teams. Secondly, policy makers are interested in increasing female participation in the auditing profession. This study's results may influence this debate (although the debate is more focused on the partner level) by showing that increasing the number of female auditors might lead to the enhancement of skepticism and thereby an improvement in audit quality.

2.8.4 Future Research and Limitations

As with every empirical study, our study has its caveats. Although we acknowledge that our sample on the intuitive and deliberate hypothesis may seem small, we have strong findings: any additional participants collected have to pass our manipulations checks on affect and on skepticism, and this will only strengthen our findings. In this study the real challenge is to find the intuitive and the deliberate auditors who exhibit professional skepticism so we can test our theory-based hypothesis. Such a challenge is often present in studies that seek to understand fundamental mechanisms behind a phenomenon, and need participants to exhibit that particular phenomenon in order to study the mechanism behind the phenomenon.[11] Although, we do not observe the auditor's brain with neuroscientific techniques (that only establish a correlational relationship between the observed brain regions and the process anyway) to infer the process behind it, this is a first empirical step toward understanding the cognitive processes behind professional skepticism and what is most likely to be the right way to proceed in setting the level of professional skepticism.

We also believe that a direct testing of a theory is novel in itself within audit research and offer a first step in guiding future researchers on how to test a theory-based hypothesis and not only hypotheses based on prior empirical findings. Indeed, experimental economics has been successful in testing theory-based hypotheses that give a unified body of findings instead of just giving a mass of unrelated empirical findings as often is observed within behavioral research on professional skepticism (Nolder and Kadous 2014).

Another limitation is that there is no optimal level of professional skepticism in this study. Finally, we do not consider client gender in our study, as has been done in some prior research (Gold et al. 2009). It may happen that our results may change if the client gender is a female. Future research on professional skepticism is warranted to explore whether client gender may influence our results.

Given the inherent limitations of experimental gender manipulation, we acknowledge that we are unable to prove causality, only associations between gender differences and the dependent variables under study. Notwithstanding these

[11]To find the auditors exhibiting System 1 and System two type of judgments has been challenging but also it is not unusual as often in other disciplines it is the only way to understand a phenomenon. See how researchers recruit the right sample to provide new knowledge related to schizophrenia (Kompus et al. 2013) on the University of Bergen website: http://www.uib.no/en/news/36390/help-hand-schizophrenics (downloaded December 5, 2014).

limitations, this study is an important step in understanding whether a greater participation of female auditors in audit teams may actually enhance professional skepticism in an audit.

Future research may support or refute our findings, using functional Magnetic Resonance Imaging (fMRI) based techniques as done by Farrell et al. (2014) will give additional evidence on the mechanism behind professionals' skepticism by relating our behavioral findings to the observed processes in the regions of auditors' brains.

References

AICPA (2002) American Institute of Certified Public Accountants (AICPA) consideration of fraud in a financial statement audit. AICPA, New York

Ball RAY (2009) Market and political/regulatory perspectives on the recent accounting scandals. J Account Res 47(2):277–323

Bhattacharjee S, Moreno K (2002) The impact of affective information on the professional judgments of more experienced and less experienced auditors. J Behav Decis Mak 15(4): 361–377

Bhattacharjee S, Moreno K, Riley T (2012) The interplay of interpersonal affect and source reliability on auditors' inventory judgments. Contemp Account Res 29(4):1087–1108

Bonner SE (2008) Judgment and decision making in accounting, 1st edn. Pearson Prentice Hall, Upper Saddle River, New Jersey

Buckless FA, Ravenscroft SP (1990) Contrast coding: a refinement of ANOVA in behavioral analysis. Account Rev 65(4):933–945

Campitelli G, Gobet F (2010) Herbert Simon's decision-making approach: investigation of cognitive processes in experts. Rev Gen Psychol 14(4):354–364

Damasio A (1994) Descartes' error: emotion, reason, and the human brain. G. P. Putnam's Sons, New York

DeFond M, Zhang J (2014) A review of archival auditing research. J Account Econ 58(2–3): 275–326

Elliott WB, Jackson KE, Peecher ME, White BJ (2013) The unintended effect of corporate social responsibility performance on investors' estimates of fundamental value. Account Rev 89(1):275–302

Farrell AM, Goh JO, White BJ (2014) The effect of performance-based incentive contracts on System 1 and System 2 processing in affective decision contexts: fMRI and behavioral evidence. Account Rev 89(6):1979–2010

Glover SM, Prawitt DF (2013) Enhancing auditor professional skepticism. Brigham Young University, Utah

Glover SM, Prawitt DF (2014) Enhancing auditor professional skepticism: The professional skepticism continuum. Curr Issues Auditing 8(2):1–10

Gold A, Hunton JE, Gomaa MI (2009) The impact of client and auditor gender on auditors' judgments. Account Horiz 23(1):1–18

Griffith EE, Hammersley JS, Kadous K (2014) Audits of complex estimates as verification of management numbers. University of Wisconsin-Madison, University of Georgia, and Emory University

Griffith EE, Hammersley JS, Kadous K, Young D (2015) Auditor mindsets and audits of complex estimates. J Account Res 53(1):47–79

Guénin-Paracini H, Malsch B, Paillé AM (2014) Fear and risk in the audit process. Acc Organ Soc 39(4):264–288
Hackenbrack K (1992) Implications of seemingly irrelevant evidence in audit judgment. J Account Res 30(1):126–136
Hurtt RK (2010) Development of a scale to measure professional skepticism. Auditing: J Pract Theor 29(1):149–171
Hurtt RK, Brown-Liburd HL, Earley CE, Krishnamoorthy G (2013) Research on auditor professional skepticism: literature synthesis and opportunities for future research. Auditing: A J Pract Theor 32(Supplement):45–97
IAASB (2012) International Accounting & Auditing Standards Board (IAASB) staff questions and answers: professional skepticism in an audit of financial statements. International Federation of Accountants (IFAC), New York
International Federation of Accountants (IFAC) (2009) International Standard on Auditing 200 (ISA 200). Overall objectives of the independent auditor and the conduct of an audit in accordance with international standards on auditing. International Federation of Accountant (IFAC), NY
Kadous K (2012) Refocusing the professional skepticism discussion: doubt versus critical thinking
Kadous K, Leiby J, Peecher ME (2013) How do auditors weight informal contrary advice? The joint influence of advisor social bond and advice justifiability. Account Rev 88(6):2061–2087
Kahneman D (2003) A perspective on judgment and choice: mapping bounded rationality. Am Psychol 58(9):697–720
Kahneman D (2011) Thinking, fast and slow. Allen Lane, London
Kida T, Moreno K, Smith JF (2001) The influence of affect on managers' capital-budgeting decisions 18(3):477–494
Knechel WR, Krishnan GV, Pevzner M, Shefchik LB, Velury UK (2012) Audit quality: insights from the academic literature. Auditing: J Practi Theor 32(Supplement 1):385–421
Kompus K, Falkenberg LE, Bless JJ, Johnsen E, Kroken RA, Kråkvik B, Larøi F, Løberg E, Vedul-Kjelsås E, Westerhausen R, Hugdahl K (2013) The role of the primary auditory cortex in the neural mechanism of auditory verbal hallucinations. Frontiers Hum Neurosci 7:144
Kunda Z (1999) Social cognition: making sense of people. The MIT Press, Cambridge
Moreno K, Kida T, Smith JF (2002) The impact of affective reactions on risky decision making in accounting contexts. J Account Res 40(5):1331–1349
Nelson MW (2009) A model and literature review of professional skepticism in auditing. Auditing: J Pract Theor 28(2):1–34
Nolder C, Kadous K (2014) The way forward on professional skepticism: Conceptualizing professional skepticism as an attitude. Suffolk University and Goizueta Business School at Emory University
PCAOB (2012) Public Company Accounting Oversight Board (PCAOB) Staff audit practice alert No. 10. Maintaining and applying professional skepticism in audits
Pike BJ, Curtis MB, Chui L (2013) How does an initial expectation bias influence auditors' application and performance of analytical procedures? Account Rev 88(4):1413–1431
Public Company Accounting Oversight Board (PCAOB) (2013) Order instituting disciplinary proceedings, making findings, and imposing sanctions. PCAOB Release No. 105-2013-009
Quadackers L (2009) A study of auditors' skeptical characteristics and their relationship to skeptical judgments and decisions. Vrije Universiteit, Amsterdam
Quadackers L, Groot T, Wright A (2014) Auditors' professional skepticism: Neutrality versus presumptive doubt. Contemp Account Res 31(3):639–657
Robertson JC (2010) The effects of ingratiation and client incentive on auditor judgment. Behav Res Account 22(2):69–86
Shaub MK (1996) Trust and suspicion: the effects of situational and dispositional factors on auditors' trust of clients. Behav Res Account 8:154–174

Slovic P, Finucane M, Petres E, MacGregor DG (2002) The affect heuristic. In: Gilovich T, Griffin D, Kahneman D (eds) Heuristics and biases. The psychology of intuitive judgment. Cambridge University Press, New York

Stanovich KE, West RF (2000) Individual differences in reasoning: implications for the rationality debate? Behav Brain Sci 23(5):645–726

Tversky A, Kahneman D (1981) The framing of decisions and the psychology of choice. Science 211(4481):453–458

Chapter 3
The Experimental Instrument

Abstract In this chapter provides a description of the experimental instrument (or questionnaire) used in the study in Chap. 2 with auditors as respondents. This chapter describes briefly the different parts in the experimental instrument as they appear in the questionnaire provided to the auditors to enable the reader to reconstruct the questionnaire if he or she wish to do so. The design in the experimental instrument manipulates the risk of material misstatement at two levels (low and high) and to manipulate affect at two levels (positive and negative). The manipulations are randomly assigned to the auditors. The experimental instrument consists of the experimental audit case that describes an ABC company, a hypothetical audit client that sells designer maternity clothing to small specialty clothing shops. The questionnaire asks the participating auditors to audit the ABC company inventory account according to the international accounting standards (IAS). The audit case in the questionnaire is based on an inventory valuation issue in ABC.

Keywords Audit client · Audit engagement · Auditor · Case · Experimental design · Experimental instrument · International accounting standard (IAS) · Inventory valuation issue · Manipulation · Material misstatements · Questionnaire

3.1 About the Experimental Instrument

In this Chapter is a kind of appendix where you will a description of the experimental instrument (or questionnaire) used in the study in Chap. 2 with auditors as respondents. This chapter describes briefly the different parts in the experimental instrument as they appear in the questionnaire provided to the auditors to enable the reader to reconstruct the questionnaire if he or she wish to do so. First, in this section you can find an overall description of the instrument. Next sections will provide a description by section of the questionnaire. While reading the descriptions, keep in mind the rest of this chapter that the participants were professional auditors asked to act as auditors in an audit firm and that the experimental instrument manipulated two factors in the audit engagement information.

C. Olsen, *A Study of Professional Skepticism*, SpringerBriefs in Accounting,
DOI 10.1007/978-3-319-49896-6_3

The design in the experimental instrument manipulates the risk of material misstatement at two levels (low and high) and to manipulate affect at two levels (positive and negative). The manipulations are randomly assigned to the auditors. The experimental instrument consists of the experimental audit case that describes an ABC company, a hypothetical company that sells designer maternity clothing to small specialty clothing shops. The ABC company is the audit client and the participating auditors are asked to audit the client. The audit case is based on an inventory valuation issue in the audit engagement ABC.

First, the instrument describes the background information about the audit client ABC and information regarding the relevant accounting standard for the audit case and the inventory valuation problem. Then, the instrument provides the participants with a set of prior year audited financial statements and current-year unaudited financial statements, and ratios for both the prior year and the current year. This information is held constant across all four conditions. After auditors have read the background information about the company, the auditors were informed either that the risk of material misstatement for the valuation assertion of inventory is low or that it is high.

Then the participants in the positive or negative affect condition received randomly either a positive affect vignette or a negative affect vignette. The affect vignettes induce auditors' affective reactions by giving auditors positive or negative information about the controller's personal characteristics. With this information, we evoke auditors' liking or disliking of the client. At this stage, participants have received both the experimental manipulations.

Then the instrument provides information relevant to the inventory business process and the likelihood of writing inventory down to net realizable value because it is lower than cost. The information about the inventory business process gives contradictory cues in such a way that the judgment in the audit task is not intrinsically clear to participants with regard to whether there is a valuation problem. The intention is to give some room for the manipulations of interpersonal affect and for situational professional skepticism to function and create variations. Although some would argue that the inventory valuation problem is very likely, auditors know that the client would prefer not to write down the inventory because a write down will influence company profitability. This makes the judgment unclear and therefore has an impact on auditors' ratings of the valuation problem.

After reading the information, auditors evaluate the likelihood that the client may have a valuation problem on a scale from 1 to 7, where 1 = Very unlikely and 7 = Very likely. This judgment measures the effect of interpersonal affect and situational professional skepticism on auditors' skeptical judgments. This is the dependent variable in the study that measures the influence of manipulating the risk and affect information in the study on auditor's skeptical judgments.

Finally, the participants received part 2 of the instrument. In part 2, participants were asked to answer manipulation check questions and demographic questions.

The manipulation check questions are used to test whether the participants have understood the different types of information on affect and risk. Then, the demographic questions asked the participants about their gender, their audit position and about their work experience. The full version of the experimental instrument into be found in the next sections. The instrument can be administrated on paper as it is or online by implementing it on a survey software.

3.2 The Experimental Instrument

3.2.1 The Audit

3.2.1.1 Accounting Standard

Under this section, the participants are instructed to act as an auditor and to read the material in the instrument. First, the participants reads the accounting standard dealing with the valuation of the inventory. The relevant accounting standard here is IAS 2 (IASB 2012). The general rule is described as following:

> According to the accounting standards, inventory is an asset held for sale in the ordinary course of business. Inventory must be revalued if the net realizable value of the inventory is lower than cost at year end.

3.2.1.2 Background of Company

The background section of the company ABC provides relevant details about the company ABC from the audit firm in the questionnaire as follows. First, ABC is a global retailer of maternity clothing that focuses on selling designer clothing to small specialty clothing shops. Your audit firm has been the auditors for ABC for the last 5 years. The company has received a clean audit opinion each year. ABC's simple and comfortable clothing design is attractive for expectant mothers. ABC believes that maternity clothing is less fashion sensitive than women's clothing in general. Although 2012 was a difficult year for the company, ABC generated a 14% increase in net income. The company's controller is responsible for inventory and has served in several positions in ABC since 2001. He has a law degree and a degree in accounting.

Second, the risk of material misstatement (i.e., control risk and inherent risk) for the ABC inventory process. In previous audits, the audit firm identified existence and valuation as relevant assertions for ABC's inventory. The audit firm attends the physical inventory count done at year end and takes test counts. In this way, they get evidence related to the existence assertion for inventory. The audit firm evaluates the valuation of inventory by reviewing sales history for each basic inventory category (casual clothing, sportswear and formal clothing) at year end.

Third, the instrument gives the participants with the first risk manipulation by providing one of the two paragraphs randomly to the participants:

The audit partner believes that the risk of material misstatement is low for the valuation assertion of inventory. The controller will revalue inventory at year end if economic or industry conditions indicate that the company may not be able to sell inventory at a sales price equal to its cost. The controller does not receive a bonus based on an increase in net income, so he has no reason to avoid revaluing inventory to net realizable value if needed.

OR

The audit partner believes that the risk of material misstatement is high for the valuation assertion of ABC's inventory. The controller does not like to write down inventory even if economic or industry conditions indicate that the company may not be able to sell inventory at a sales price equal to its cost. The controller receives a bonus if net income increases by 13%. In the past, he has used the estimate of inventory obsolescence to make sure that net income increases by the amount needed so he get his bonus.

Then the instrument provides narrative from the partner's briefing with the audit team. In the planning meeting. During the planning meeting, the audit partner commented on his prior experience with the company. In this part, the instrument gives the participants with the second experimental manipulation (i.e., the affect manipulation) by providing one of the two paragraphs randomly to the participants:

According to the partner, "ABC's success has made the controller very arrogant and difficult to deal with. Last year, I remember one time Mike Jenkins, one of our seniors, wanted to meet with the controller to get some information on the inventory system. The controller has a good reputation in the industry and really knows what he is doing. But he refuses to work with the audit staff. Last year the controller refused to meet the audit senior, saying that he was too busy. It was not as if the controller was trying to hide anything. I had several meetings with him during this time, and he was always very cooperative. He just did not want to take the time to talk to someone at a lower level in the audit firm".

OR

According to the partner, "The company has been very successful and the controller is easy to work with. Last year, Mike Jenkins, one of our audit seniors, wanted to meet with the controller to get some information on their inventory system. The controller has a good reputation in the industry and really knows what he is doing. He was happy to explain the system to Mike Jenkins. The controller repeatedly met Mike saying that he was always available whenever he needed to speak with him. I also had several meetings with the controller during this time and he was always very cooperative".

3.2.2 *Inventory Business Process*

This section of the questionnaire provides the participants with detail information on ABC inventory. Exhibit 3.1. portrays this part of the questionnaire. The detail information about the ABC inventory consists of the valuation policy for ABC inventories, the income statements for two consequent years, the average cost and selling price per item of goods in the inventory and other key financial trends related to the ABC inventory. The end of this part provides information about the market to provide uncertainty about the inventory status because this will lead to variation in participants' judgments of the inventory valuation problem.

Exhibit 3.1. Working papers for 2012 (unaudited) and 2011 (audited)
A. ABC's accounting policy:

Inventories are required to be stated at the lower of cost and net realizable value [IAS 2.9]. Cost is determined in ABC using the weighted average cost method. Net realizable value is estimated as the selling price of the item in the ordinary course of business. Any write-downs to net realizable value should be recognized as an expense in the period in which the write-down occurs.

B. Income statements for 2011–2012—in millions $:

	Current year unaudited 2012	Previous year audited 2011	Change	Percent (%)
Revenues/sales	72	76	−4	−5
Cost of goods sold	50	53	−3	−6
Gross profit	22	23	−1	−4
Selling, general and administrative expense	14	16	−2	−13
Operating income	8	7	1	14

C. Average cost per item: $42.
D. Average selling price per item: $50.
E. Five year summary:

	2012	2011	2010	2009	2008
Inventories (in millions)	13	12	11	13	14
Inventories turnover	4	5	6	6	6
Revenues (in millions)	72	76	76	81	83
Gross profit	22	23	23	24	26
Gross profit %	30%	30%	30%	30%	31%

F. Information about inventory status:

The controller explained the inventory changes in 2012 as follows: ABC is facing a new global competitor OHO who established a low price maternity clothing brand in mid-2011. According to OHO's press release in December 2011, OHO advertised an average selling price of $40 per item. This is lower than ABC's average selling price of $50 per item. ABC believes that it may have either to reduce its selling price to $40 in 2013 or compete with OHO by advertising a higher quality product. The controller has not written the inventory down because the company has not made the final decision about which of the two alternatives to follow.

3.2.3 Audit Task

Based on the information that the auditors have read, the audit task section asks the auditors to indicate the likelihood that the client may have a valuation problem. This means that auditors indicates the likelihood that the where the client inventory should be written-down. The auditors indicate the likelihood on a 7-point scale as shown in Exhibit 3.2. Next under this section, an open-ended question asks the auditors to provide the major factor(s) or evidence that they considered when making their decisions about whether the client had a valuation problem.

Exhibit 3.2. Seven-point scale of likelihood

- Very Unlikely
- Unlikely
- Somewhat Unlikely
- Undecided
- Somewhat Likely
- Likely
- Very Likely.

3.2.4 Other Questions

Subsequent to the audit task, auditors answers five manipulation check questions. In experimental instruments, the researcher will ask the participants questions to test whether they payed attention to the experimental manipulations in the experimental instrument. In this instrument, the manipulation check questions are intended to check whether the auditors payed attention to the experimental manipulations of risk and affect. Exhibit 3.3. below shows the first four questions interrogating the auditors about their feelings toward the client's controller behavior. These four questions test whether the auditors have payed attention to the affect manipulation. Then the fifth question is intended to test whether the auditors have payed attention to the risk (i.e., a proxy for skepticism) manipulation. The auditors answer these questions on a seven point scale from strongly disagree to strongly agree as shown below.

Exhibit 3.3. Manipulation check
Please indicate whether you agree with following statements:

1. **I like the client's controller.**

- Strongly Disagree
- Disagree
- Somewhat Disagree
- Neither Agree nor Disagree
- Somewhat Agree
- Agree
- Strongly Agree.

2. **I am frustrated with client's controller.**

- Strongly Disagree
- Disagree
- Somewhat Disagree
- Neither Agree nor Disagree
- Somewhat Agree
- Agree
- Strongly Agree.

3. **I am happy with the client's controller.**

- Strongly Disagree
- Disagree
- Somewhat Disagree
- Neither Agree nor Disagree
- Somewhat Agree
- Agree
- Strongly Agree.

4. **I am irritated with client's controller.**

- Strongly Disagree
- Disagree
- Somewhat Disagree
- Neither Agree nor Disagree
- Somewhat Agree
- Agree
- Strongly Agree.

5. **The client's controller has a strong motivation to manipulate short term results.**

- Strongly Disagree
- Disagree
- Somewhat Disagree
- Neither Agree nor Disagree

- Somewhat Agree
- Agree
- Strongly Agree.

3.2.5 Demographic Questions

This section is the final section of the instrument. The questions map auditors' background and figure under the title demographic questions in the instrument. Demographic questions ask the auditors about their gender, their audit position, years of audit experience, the current employer, and how much audit experience they have within inventory valuation. After answering those questions, the auditors have read through the whole instrument and have finished answering the instrument.

Reference

International Accounting Standards Board (IASB) (2012) IAS 2 Inventories technical summary

Kolibri 360 GmbH
Ferdinand-Jühlke-Straße 7
99095 Erfurt, Deutschland
produktsicherheit@kolibri360.de